True or False Possession?

Jean Lhermitte

True or False Possession?

How to Distinguish
the Demonic from the Demented

Edited by Aaron Kheriaty, MD

SOPHIA INSTITUTE PRESS
Manchester, New Hampshire

True or False Possession?, an English translation by P. J. Hepburne-Scott of *Vrais et faux possédés* (F. Brouty, J. Fayard, et Cie, 1956), was originally published in 1963 by Hawthorn Books, New York, as Volume 43 of the *Twentieth Century Encyclopedia of Catholicism*, edited by Henri Daniel-Rops. This 2013 edition by Sophia Institute Press includes minor editorial revisions and a new preface.

Nihil obstat: Joannes M. T. Barton, S.T.D., L.S.S., *Censor Deputatus*
Imprimatur: E. Morrogh Bernard, *Vicarius Generalis*,
Westmonasterii, December 13, 1962

Sophia Institute Press
Box 5284, Manchester, NH 03108
1-800-888-9344

www.SophiaInstitute.com

Sophia Institute Press® is a registered trademark of Sophia Institute.

Library of Congress Cataloging-in-Publication Data

Lhermitte, Jean, 1877-1959.
    [Vrais et faux possedes. English]
    True or false possession? : How to distinguish the demonic from the demented / Jean Lhermitte ; edited by Aaron Kheriaty.
        pages cm
    "True and False Possession, an English translation by P. J. Hepburned Scott of Vrais et faux possedes (F. Brouty, J. Fayard, et Cie, 1956), was originally published in 1963 by Hawthorn Books, New York, as Volume 43 of the Twentieth Century Encyclopedia of Catholicism, edited by Henri Daniel-Rops."
    Includes bibliographical references.
    ISBN 978-1-933184-89-0 (pbk. : alk. paper) 1. Demoniac possession.
I. Kheriaty, Aaron. II. Title.
    BF1555.L553 2013
    133.4'26 — dc23
                                                            2013018313

First printing

Contents

Preface

by Aaron Kheriaty, MD

The question about the devil was put to me directly by a patient who had come to see me for treatment of depression and recovery from a serious drug addiction. As a physician, he had gained access to the intravenous anesthetic drug propofol and had self-administered it in order to escape from refractory insomnia and unrelenting depression. Without carefully titrated dosing, gleaned from his medical knowledge, this patient would surely have overdosed long ago. Indeed, it was something of a miracle that he was still alive.

During an interview, he suddenly interrupted the narrative of his psychiatric history, paused, and looked me directly in the eye. With a sober seriousness, and without a trace of hysterics or dramatization, he asked simply, "Do you believe in the Devil?"

I stared back. "Yes. I do."

"Me too," he said.

Then after a pause, I inquired: "Why do you ask?"

"When I was injecting the propofol I felt something . . . enter into me. It was not the drug, but something else. The drug was just the gateway. It was . . . something . . . foreign."

True or False Possession?

At no point in his treatment did I suspect this patient to be possessed, in the strict sense of the term. Yet, neither did I doubt the reality of a malevolent influence on him that exceeded in power and scope the physiological effects of the anesthetic he was abusing. He later related to me how this evil spirit would mock and taunt him as he slipped deeper into the hell of drug addiction.

Most of my colleagues in psychiatry probably would have regarded this exchange between doctor and patient as rather puzzling, even ludicrous. They would likewise regard a book like the one you hold here as an oddity. A work purporting to distinguish between cases of true and false possession will seem to many a throwback to a bygone age of religious superstition. Yet a modern psychiatrist cannot help but be impressed by the author's perspicuous medical and psychological analysis of each case he examines in these pages. This is not the work of a premodern credulous dupe, but the work of a skilled and experienced neurologist, who knows his trade and sees his way clearly into the tangled workings of the human mind and heart.

The author, a physician and not a theologian, skillfully navigates the Scylla of credulity and the Charybdis of relentless skepticism. Inclined by training and clinical experience to search first for naturalistic medical or psychiatric explanations for the phenomena in question, he nevertheless leaves open the possibility of explanations that go beyond what science or medicine can assess, as well as the possibility that any given manifestation may have elements of both the natural and preternatural. Originally published over fifty years ago, the author's medical judgments and observations still hold true. While some clinical terminology may have changed in the interim, little could be brought to bear from modern neurology or psychiatry that would contradict his findings or conclusions. The clinical histories, fascinating in their own right aside from the author's clinical assessment, are presented with sober clarity and reserve.

Believers have sometimes made the mistake of finding supernatural possession where there was only a pathological personality, given to the grossest hysterics and deceptions. This book provides fascinating accounts of false-possession cases, for example, those of Marie-Thérèse Noblet and Sr. Jeanne of the Angels. Here the author astutely notes that the repeated misapplication of the Rite of Exorcism may have exacerbated the behavioral disorder, in this case, hysterical (what we now call conversion) symptoms that were encouraged by the excessive attention received from the exorcist and by the public or overly dramatized way in which the exorcist misapplied the rite, in defiance of the prescriptions of the Roman Ritual. The curious onlookers fell prey to the colorful and dramatic, while the sick individual was motivated by receiving such attention. The author observes: "Well known, too, were all the criteria which the Church holds to be decisive of genuine possession, but they were scarcely heeded" in such cases. The cautionary note here comes not from a belief that the rite or the prayers themselves would be harmful, but rather from a desire to avoid an overly theatrical application of a sacramental in situations where the hysterical person was taking on the sick role precisely in order to draw attention to herself. The author discerns that it was the excessive attention, not the prayers of the rite itself, that could have exacerbated the behavioral symptoms.

In a similar vein, the author then recounts well-documented historical cases of mass hysteria and pseudoseizures, which often become "contagious" among those living in close quarters through suggestion and mimesis. Such phenomena could be accounted for by psychological observations known as early as the sixteenth century and given more definitive form in the work of the great French neurologist Charcot in the nineteenth century. Today, one could add a wider knowledge of culture-bound syndromes worldwide, with characteristically wild behavioral, dissociative, and somatic manifestations—such as the clinical syndrome Amok found among the Malaysians. In such cases, as the author concludes, "the influence of the demon is to be sought in vain." Yet he also notes correctly that hysteria is not playacting and that those who manifested this behavioral disorder were not consciously feigning their symptoms or deliberately trying to deceive: "Hysterical patients, like all other sick people, deserve our understanding and our charity."

The author knows well that some historical cases, thought at the time to be demonic possession, can now be explained as having their origin in neurological or psychiatric disorders. Yet he displays none of the hubris of modern men who scoff at the superstitions of past ages, as though they had made such medical discoveries themselves. He writes with sympathy for the limited theories employed by men of the past, even while correcting their errors or misjudgments in particular cases. He is also careful to point out that there were contemporaneous skeptics, who, although they could not offer alternative explanations, nonetheless had the insight to doubt the presence of true demoniacal influence where there was none. In the case of false possessions where an exorcism was mistakenly employed, the author offers this psychologically penetrating insight, which rests upon the mechanism of projection: "It must be remembered that if one calls up the devil, one will see, not the devil himself, but a portrait composed according to the patient's idea of him."

Preface

By the time our author takes the reader through chapters 3 and 4, explaining in light of modern neurological and psychiatric concepts what were at the time riotously incomprehensible manifestations and behaviors, and disabusing the reader of any supernatural interpretation of these cases of pseudo-possession, one is left wondering whether all apparent demonic manifestations can be likewise explained away or accounted for by naturalistic explanations. With astute medical insight, the author describes a case of postpartum depression with psychotic features, including homicidal command-type auditory hallucinations: "One of my patients, for example, during a state of depression heard the devil in the middle of the night speaking to her and bidding her kill her child, then a few months old." After acting on this impulse and tragically tossing the poor child out the window (fortunately the baby was only bruised), she received medical treatment and made a good recovery: "As for the mother, when she had been given electric shock treatment, she was not long in recovering her mental equilibrium." Naturalistic explanations for such evil sensory perceptions and violent acts can often be found within the realm of well-described mental illnesses.

In light of such cases, a skeptical reader might wonder whether the Latin Rite of Major Exorcism should now be tossed into the dustbin? Is it the product of a bygone era, now known to be defunct and discredited by the findings of modern science and medicine? Have psychoanalytic concepts, or modern materialistic theories of the mind sufficiently disabused us of the need for supernatural explanations, for recourse to angels and demons? As our author poses the question, "If there can be no doubt of the existence of non-genuine possessions, are we in a position to distinguish them from the genuine?" But even while he goes about the work of debunking, he is also spiritually astute enough to avoid throwing the baby out with the bathwater. The misuse of something like the Rite of Exorcism does not negate its proper and sometimes necessary use.

We still face this question: How do we account for the manifestations documented in many cases that were thoroughly examined by competent psychiatrists, cases still seen today that evade the explanations of skilled physicians? Can modern psychiatry or neurology give an account of all such things — of preternatural knowledge, of superhuman strength, of xenoglossia, of inexplicable rage toward sacred objects — or will science ever discover a naturalistic cause here? I have observed firsthand several of these demonic manifestations during an exorcism, manifestations for which I can find no explanation within the realm of natural science.

This book needs to be framed in the context of profound cultural shifts that have occurred since it was first published in 1956, most notably the rise of a widespread philosophy of materialism that turns appreciation for science into an ideological scientism. Such secularizing cultural changes surely influence the book's readership. When the author wrote it, he could assume that most Catholic readers would, by and large, take for granted the necessity of exorcism in certain cases and not doubt its efficacy in instances of true possession. He was writing therefore with the prudent intent to avoid overzealous applications of the rite in cases that had not been sufficiently medically examined. But the background cultural assumptions today are radically different, even among many Catholics, including many clergy. Today the default assumption for many readers would be that naturalistic or medical explanations can always be found and can be taken as fully explanatory. The danger today is therefore precisely the opposite, namely, that the rite may now be under-applied rather than overused. Indeed, in many dioceses in the United States there is no available trained exorcist to deal with such cases, and afflicted individuals therefore suffer without recourse.

This author knows the permanent limitations of his science: this book does not attempt to detail cases of what may be considered true possession, for these by their nature would lie outside the scope of the author's explanatory powers or clinical expertise. That task is best left to the trained and experienced exorcist and to the theologian. Where the physician has reached the limits of his methods, where medical or psychological explanations simply cannot account for the phenomena, then the doctor must recognize the boundaries of his own craft and remain silent before the mystery of iniquity — the mystery of a real and effective evil personality that in rare cases may oppress and torment some few unfortunate souls.

In such cases the physician and the priest need to collaborate responsibly, and with respect for the insights of both science and theology. Fr. Gary Thomas, who is the subject of journalist Matt Baglio's book, *The Rite: The Making of a Modern Exorcist*, later adapted for the Hollywood film by the same name, starring Anthony Hopkins, recently recounted to me severe cases of demonic possession with extraordinary manifestations. Some of these I have since witnessed during an exorcism and can attest that such "symptoms" lie outside the scope of anything listed in the psychiatrist's *Diagnostic and Statistical Manual of Mental Disorders*. Fr. Gary also gave me an invaluable insight into his work when he explained that an exorcism is always an act of healing. And so, of course, the Church recognizes the urgent need for competent neurologists and psychiatrists to work with exorcists in the process of discernment, diagnostics, treatment, and healing. But such collaboration presumes that each person—both the medical doctor and the priest exorcist—have something indispensable to contribute to this work of discernment and healing. This is a work of mercy, patterned after our Lord's own acts of casting out demons and curing disease.

Introduction

by Henri Daniel-Rops

It may perhaps surprise the reader to learn that the author of this work is a neurologist, not a theologian. States of possession, he may say, whether real or simulated by sickness, are surely, by their very structure, the concern of theology and the field of the exorcist.

The argument has weight, and we must be careful not to underestimate it. But while in earlier days, when supposedly diabolical possessions were so numerous, the exorcist was almost the sole judge, nowadays our knowledge in the field of normal and pathological psychology has advanced tremendously, especially since the nineteenth century, when psychiatry freed itself from the mists of a philosophy without natural foundations and really became a science based on observation and criticism.

There is no doubt that states of demoniacal possession or obsession are still extremely frequent, and scarcely a month passes without some example being brought to my own notice.

No, whatever skeptics, unbelievers, and the ill-informed may think, demonopathic manifestations are not extinct; we still observe the phenomena that startled and alarmed our forefathers, but with a critical sense and knowledge that they did not possess. But I must make it clear that while the neurologist and the psychiatrist are qualified to discern and define an abnormal structure of the mind or some bodily disorder, they should remain physicians and not exceed their powers, so that in cases where mental illness is not clearly present the neuropsychiatrist ought to call in the help and cooperation of the theologian. I believe that I have not myself failed in this duty, and the majority of my personal observations have been checked by qualified persons.

This book will quite certainly be criticized by believers and nonbelievers alike, but while I accept in advance the most severe strictures, I would ask the reader to consider it dispassionately, for it has been written with objectivity and in all good faith.

Although it is currently maintained that cases of diabolical possession appeared more frequently in an age when religious faith was more vigorous than today, observation of the facts proves otherwise: people who profess to be possessed by the devil are very far from rare. I should add that I am here envisaging only the western Catholic world to which we belong and that we could not justifiably extend this assertion to other peoples whose religion and customs are different.

All the same, every writer on the subject has remarked that the phenomenon of possession has never been confined to one epoch or to one particular milieu. The picture of "diabolical possession" certainly seems to be more frequent in primitive societies, while it appears in other colors among civilized peoples, among whom science has torn away the fallacious mask of a certain popular image of the devil; but, for all that, even in very developed societies, belief in the influence of the materialized devil, and his entry into the body of certain men marked down by fate, remains very much alive.

But first of all, are we sure of the real existence of an "unclean spirit," an "evil spirit" who prowls around us, seeking whom he may devour? There can be no Christian who does not give an affirmative answer to this question. The Church teaches it through the mouth of her greatest Doctors, and among them Bossuet. That great shepherd of souls, whose depth, lucidity and breadth of judgment can never be too highly praised, was so haunted by the fear that Christian souls might lose their horror of the devil, that he devoted two sermons to this theme. In the first, Bossuet proclaims: "Just as a pestilent vapor is hidden in the air and, imperceptible to our senses, insinuates its poison into our hearts, so this malignant spirit, by a subtle and imperceptible contagion, corrupts the purity of our souls. We do not suspect that he is acting in us, because he follows the current of our inclinations. He presses us and overthrows us on the side to which he sees we are leaning."[1]

What the preacher is warning us against is the subtle and noxious influence of the diabolical spirit, which we do not see or feel, precisely because he acts in accordance with the bent of our passions and inclinations. On this point, at least, Bossuet was in agreement with Baudelaire, who maintained that "the devil's greatest cunning is to make us think he does not exist." We must, then, admit that certain persons allow the devil's evil influence to enter them without their being aware of it.

In the Church, the devil was long considered simply as the unclean spirit, the tempter, the evil one, of whom it was

---

[1] Jacques-Bénigne Bossuet, Sermons preached on the First Sunday in Lent 1656 and on the First Sunday in Lent 1660.

necessary to beware because of his dissembling, his skill in deception, and his strength, that power which Bossuet so strongly emphasizes. From a careful study of history, at least in the West, it appears that it was in the thirteenth century that diabolical manifestations began to be more violent, more singular, and more widespread. But, while the devil's supposed action took on more extraordinary forms, he himself at the same time assumed a body, materialized himself. The possessed person was no longer simply a being animated with "diabolical" thoughts or impulses; he believed himself to be penetrated in mind and even in body by the devil. He saw him, heard him, perceived him with all his senses; observers even attributed bodily marks to the malice of the devil—ecchymoses, wounds, burns, a whole catalogue of manifestations, whose organic nature could not be doubted.

As we might guess, faced with phenomena so strange and usually so very dramatic, certain critical minds were disturbed and expressly raised the question: How can we know whether these so-called possessions do not conceal mental diseases?

Although the science of mental illness was still in its infancy (for scientific psychiatry dates only from the beginning of the nineteenth century), the good sense of certain religious and the discernment of some doctors had already relegated the vagaries of the pseudo-possessed to the sphere of pathology. In this connection, the case of Marthe Brossier is very significant. This woman, accepted by the exorcists and by Bérulle[2] himself as a genuine case of possession, was unable to withstand a clinical examination by an experienced doctor, Marescot, appointed

---

[2] Pierre de Bérulle (1575-1629), cardinal and founder of the French Congregation of the Oratory.

by Henri IV. This clinician, who behaved in this affair with an acumen and discernment that merit the utmost admiration, demolished Marthe's claims to possession by the devil and also the myth of a "supernatural state," which her theatrical demonstrations appeared to support.

Nowadays no one doubts the existence of cases of pseudo-possession, that is, of the mentally sick whose singular behavior can be rationally interpreted.

Is it legitimate to speak of "spurious possession"?

But before penetrating to the heart of our subject, two questions arise that must be answered, if we are to be allowed to use such terms as *spurious possession*. First, do such expressions contain a contradiction? Spurious possession is not possession at all; it is only a disease. According to this view, we can speak only of genuine possession.

We may note that this criticism has already been leveled against authors who have used the term *false mystics* to contrast them with *genuine mystics*. To this we may reply that the Gospel itself warns us against the false prophets who are contrasted with the genuine [cf. Matt. 7:15-20] and that, with the pseudo-mystics, as with the pseudo-demoniacs, what calls for attention and investigation is precisely the fact that certain persons display the deceptive appearances of the genuine mystic or the genuinely possessed.

And the severest critics are not slow to claim that the task of distinguishing preternatural states, whether divine or diabolical, from behavior that can be explained by the action of natural forces often bristles with difficulties. I may therefore be allowed to retain the term *spurious possession* or *pseudo-demoniacal* to define our subject, when such definition is necessary.

The second question requiring an answer concerns the lawfulness of the doctor's intervention in the discernment of the pseudo-diabolical. How, one may ask, can a doctor, be he ever so skilled in medicine and psychiatry, presume to judge of states that lie outside his province and are the field of the theologian and the exorcist? Precisely, I answer, because the qualified doctor possesses knowledge on the pathology of the mind which the theologian and the exorcist cannot command.

Observation of these cases of spurious possession has shown that these states correspond very closely with mental afflictions that are perfectly well defined and can therefore be identified with certainty by the medical specialist. The structure of the "psychological neo-formation" of demonopathic delirium, or the picture of a neuropathic state on a demoniacal theme, are the same as those more commonly observed, but with a different content. This is so true that in either case one can predict the course of the disease, estimate the prognosis, and prescribe its treatment. There is therefore nothing surprising in the fact that the number of so-called "demoniacal possessions" decreases as psychiatry becomes more penetrating and more comprehensive.

On the other hand, all the studies bearing on our subject have shown that it is impossible to include under one description all the facts of demonopathy, for the forms under which it appears are quite varied. Without prejudging the causal mechanism, we may class the facts of demonopathy or spurious possession in two main groups: those which are manifested intermittently or in explosive paroxysms, and those which, being better disguised, follow a development which is all the more deceptive in that it does not necessarily modify the behavior of the "possessed" in a very visible manner.[3]

[3] As there is no convenient English equivalent for "pseudo-possession" etc. and the great majority of cases mentioned in this book belong to that category, the terms *possession, possessed*, etc. are used for the non-genuine state, except where it is clearly stated or implied by the context that the possession is genuine. *Who Is the Devil?*, by Nicolas Corte [New York: Hawthorn Books, 1958; Manchester, New Hampshire: Sophia Institute Press, 2013], mentions some of the cases dealt with by the present work. While the facts of these cases are not generally in dispute between Dr. Lhermitte and Mr. Corte, their interpretations of them are often at variance.

True or False Possession?

Chapter 1

Genuine Demoniacal Possession

Any such term as *spurious possession* necessarily implies the idea of a genuine possession of a human being by the evil one, and critical minds have not failed to ask what are the distinguishing marks of such genuine diabolical possession.

I am not, of course, a theologian, and I shall not presume to venture into a field which is not mine but the exorcist's. But I cannot evade the question so often put to me: do you really believe in the existence of demoniacal possession?

As a Christian I can only answer that I do. The role of the devil is so often asserted in the Scriptures—in the Gospels, in the Acts of the Apostles, in the letters of St. Paul, and in the Old Testament—that it is impossible to doubt it.

In the Synoptic Gospels the term *demon* appears more often in Mark than in Matthew, but every one of the authors of the first three Gospels expressly mentions the existence of a being whom they call, in varying circumstances, the "wicked spirit," the "unclean spirit," the "demon," or the "devil." Persons who are subjected to the power of this spirit are described as "demonized." Edward Langton, in his classic work, *The Essentials of Demonology*, pertinently reminds us that the word *devil* is more restricted than *demon*. The devil, in fact, is the prince of the demons, the chief of the wicked spirits; he is Satan.

But whether it is Satan, the chief of the demons, or one of the thousands of other "evil" beings, their influence always appears as pernicious, although this does not necessarily mean that it is morally harmful.

The demon can afflict a person's body without thereby making him sinful. According to Langton, what differentiates the book of Revelation from the content of the Gospels is that in the former the accent is on the moral aspect of the possession, whereas the Synoptics present the demons rather as the cause of physical sufferings. Moreover, the possessed are often represented as the unfortunate derelicts of mankind: dumb, imbecile, subject to convulsions, but not necessarily blameworthy. Even the fever that afflicted Peter's mother-in-law seemed to be attributable to the malign influence of some demon [cf. Matt. 8:14 ff.; Mark 1:30 ff.].

The Gospels describe with particular emphasis the miraculous cures performed by Jesus on those who came to Him, or on the sick recommended to Him by those who had faith in Him and His divine mission. One day, St. Luke tells us, they brought to Him all who were sick or tormented by various pains and diseases, demoniacs, lunatics, and paralytics, "and he cured them" [Matt. 4:24].

"When it was evening," we read in St. Mark, "and the sun went down, they brought to him all those who were afflicted, and those who were possessed by devils; so that the whole city stood crowding there at the door. And he healed many that were afflicted with diseases of every sort, and cast out many devils; to the devils he would give no leave to speak, because they recognized him" [cf. Mark 1:32-34].

This passage should be carefully pondered. What is so important in it? Just this: that Jesus delivered the sick from the diseases that afflicted them and drove out the demons from the bodies of the wretches possessed by them, charging the demons "not to speak, because they recognized him."

We thus learn from the opening pages of the Synoptic Gospels that among the crowds of sufferers who thronged Him and implored His help, our Lord distinguished the sick from the possessed.

If we rightly interpret the sense of the Gospel narrative, we conclude that Jesus held that genuine diseases could be caused by the intrusion of one or several demons into a man's physical and moral personality. But the cure of sickness in its pure state, if we may call it so, would be worked in a different way from the expulsion of an "evil spirit." We can prove this from the sudden cure of a child (Mark 9:13-28).

> When He reached His disciples, He found a great multitude gathered around them and some of the scribes disputing with them. The multitude, as soon as they saw Him, were overcome with awe, and ran up to welcome Him. He asked them, "What is the dispute you are holding among you?" And one of the multitude answered, "Master, I have brought my son to thee; he is possessed by a dumb spirit, and wherever it seizes on him, it tears him, and he foams at the mouth, and gnashes his teeth, and his strength is drained from him. And I bade thy disciples cast it out, but they were powerless." And he answered them, "Ah, faithless generation, how long must I be with you, how long must I bear with you? Bring him to me."

So they brought the boy to him, and the evil spirit, as soon as it saw him, threw the boy into a convulsion, so that he fell on the ground, writhing and foaming at the mouth.

And now Jesus asked the father, "How long has this been happening to him?" "From childhood," he said, "and often it has thrown him into the fire, and into water, to make an end of him. Come, have pity on us, and help us, if thou canst." But Jesus said to him, "If thou canst believe, to him who believes, everything is possible." Whereupon the father of the boy cried aloud, in tears, "Lord, I do believe; succour my unbelief."

And Jesus, seeing how the multitude was gathering round them, rebuked the unclean spirit: "Thou dumb and deaf spirit," he said, "it is I that command thee: come out of him, and never enter into him again." With that, crying aloud and throwing him into a violent convulsion, it came out of him, and he lay there like a corpse, so that many declared, "He is dead." But Jesus took hold of his hand, and raised him, and he stood up.

When he had gone into a house, and they were alone, the disciples asked him, "Why was it that we could not cast it out?" And he told them, "There is no way of casting out such spirits as this except by prayer and fasting."

St. Mark's description of the boy's convulsions, as well as the very special circumstances surrounding such a "spectacular" sight, so gratifying to the curiosity of the crowd, leave us in no doubt that here we have a case of the "falling sickness," convulsive epilepsy. Now, while convulsions of this type have been seen with the utmost frequency throughout the ages and in all civilizations, we are still very far from knowing their radical origin in many cases.

And if we admit the existence of a demoniacal influence, there is nothing to prevent us from believing that the "wicked spirit" is capable of so acting on a man's body as to produce symptoms very similar to, or even identical with, those which all doctors attribute to some organic lesion.

Other cases of possession by the evil one are described in a manner that might be thought similar to the above, but are actually quite different. For an example, we quote the event recorded by St. Mark (1:21-27):

> So they made their way to Capharnaum; here, as soon as the sabbath came, he went into the synagogue and taught; and they were amazed by his teaching, for he sat there teaching them like one who had authority, not like the scribes. And there, in the synagogue, was a man possessed by an unclean spirit, who cried aloud: "Why dost thou meddle with us, Jesus of Nazareth? Hast thou come to make an end of us? I recognize thee for what thou art, the Holy One of God." Jesus spoke to him threateningly: "Silence!" he said; "come out of him." Then the unclean spirit threw him into a convulsion, and cried with a loud voice, and so came out of him.
>
> All were full of astonishment. "What can this be?" they asked one another. "What is this new teaching? See how he has authority to lay his commands even on the unclean spirits, and they obey him!"

Without presuming to state positively the nature of the convulsive agency which took hold of the possessed man when our Lord ordered the unclean spirit to come out of him, we can assert that in this case epilepsy cannot be the cause of it. The incidence of the symptoms and their development appear quite differently.

It is always very instructive to read the Gospel stories attentively, and especially the Gospel of St. Mark, for these stories show us that while the possessed man may have the notion of his affliction, he does not imagine the "demon" in a visible form, as do so many modern cases of possession. What distinguishes the possessed from the normal person is chiefly his behavior. On this point the story in St. Mark (5:1-15) of the deliverance at Gerasa is full of instruction:

> So they came to the further shore of the sea, in the country of the Gerasenes.[4] And as soon as he had disembarked, a man possessed by an unclean spirit came out of the rock tombs to meet him. This man made his dwelling among the tombs, and nobody could keep him bound any longer, even with chains. He had been bound with fetters and chains often before, but had torn the chains apart and broken the fetters, and nobody had the strength to control him. Thus he spent all his time, night and day, among the tombs and the hills, crying aloud and cutting himself with stones. When he saw Jesus from far off, he ran up and fell at his feet, and cried with a loud voice, "Why dost thou meddle with me, Jesus, Son of the most high God? I adjure thee in God's name, do not torment me" (for he was saying, "Come out of the man, thou unclean spirit"). Then he asked him, "What is thy name?" The spirit told him, "My name is Legion;

---

[4] On the borders of Perea and Arabia.

there are many of us," and it was full of entreaties that he would not send them away out of the country. There, at the foot of the mountain, was a great herd of swine feeding; and the devils entreated him, "Send us into the swine, let us make our lodging there." With that, Jesus gave them leave; and the unclean spirits came out, and went into the swine; whereupon the herd rushed down at full speed into the sea, some two thousand in number, and the sea drowned them. The swineherds fled, and told their news in the city and in the countryside; so that they came out to see what had befallen; and when they reached Jesus, they found the possessed man sitting there, clothed and restored to his wits, and they were overcome with fear.

It appears then, from the teaching of the Gospels, that the demons have a particular liking for dry and desert spots, for tombs or places which are the haunt of wild beasts, but the evil spirit does not appear to the possessed man as something alien to himself, or under the form of a repulsive or dangerous animal. In the incident of Gerasa, it is permissible to think that the desperate flight of the swine may have been caused by the man's gesticulations at the moment of his exorcism.

In the final analysis, what general lessons can we draw from the reading of the Gospels, and especially the Synoptics? (The fourth Gospel is much more reserved about demoniacal manifestations.)

One of the most striking features is the outward transformation of the personality. Scripture teaches us that it is indeed the demon which speaks through the mouth of the possessed person; it is always the demon itself that Jesus rebukes. Everything therefore tends to make us believe that for the subject's own personality there is substituted an alien personality, dominating and exclusive, that is, the demon.

But that is not all, for the possessed person seems to be gifted with knowledge and powers not his own: he speaks with tongues unknown to himself, or imaginary; his voice, his outward appearance, are totally transformed; further, he divines hidden things, discerns spirits and recognizes Jesus as the Son of God.

We note that Jesus invariably commanded the possessed man, and therefore the demon, not to reveal who Jesus was and with what mission He was charged, So we read in St. Mark about the cure of the demoniac who asked Him: "Why dost thou meddle with us?... I recognize thee for what thou art, the Holy One of God." But Jesus threatened him: "Silence! Come out of him."

A little later, describing the cure of many sick people and the setting free of others who were possessed, the Evangelist writes: "He healed many that were afflicted with diseases of every sort, and cast out many devils; to the devils he would give no leave to speak, because they recognized him" [Mark 1:34].

In the chapter about the twelve Apostles, St. Mark records other identical incidents: "He did many works of healing, so that all those who were visited with suffering thrust themselves upon him, to touch him. The unclean spirits, too, whenever they saw him, used to fall at his feet and cry out, 'Thou art the Son of God'; and he would give them a strict charge not to make him known" [Mark 3:10-12].

We find just the same teaching in the other Synoptics, but it is noteworthy that while the demons speak with the mouth of the possessed and claim to recognize Jesus' divinity, they never praise or worship Him, in contrast with a certain possessed man of later days, whose curious and unhappy story we shall have to relate.

Before concluding this chapter, we think it worth recalling that a possessed person can be delivered from a distance, without Jesus even seeing the unfortunate patient. This is borne out by the story of the Canaanite woman in St. Mark (7:27-30). A Gentile, a Syrophoenician (and therefore probably a pagan), she begged our Lord to cast the devil out of her daughter. But Jesus said to her: "'Let the children have their fill first; it is not right to take the children's bread and throw it to the dogs.' She answered him, 'Ah, yes, Lord: the dogs eat of the crumbs the children leave, underneath the table.' And he said to her, 'In reward for this word of thine, back home with thee; the devil has left thy daughter.' And when she came back to her house, she found her daughter lying on the bed, and the devil gone."

To account for facts of this kind we must therefore admit that Jesus knew the state of this possessed child without having seen it and also that the power of the divine exorcist could extend to those who were completely ignorant of his personality. There is here no room for the hypothesis so often invoked for the casting out of demons: either a miraculous cure by suggestion or the effect of faith.

Satan in the New Testament

As indicated at the beginning of this work, our reading of the Scriptures forbids us to confuse Satan with "the demon." The latter, as he has shown on many occasions, is Legion, "many." Satan is unique. He is the prince, the head of the demons. But it seems that Satan's influence appears as more subtle, more spiritual, than that of the demons, whose activity, as I have emphasized, is very violent or at least somewhat rough. The part played by Satan in man's mind is undoubtedly more obscure, more disguised, and all the more pernicious, but against his influence man can and must defend himself. And while Jesus and his disciples have nothing but pity for the demoniacs, the subjects of Satan are harshly rebuked. We recall the episode of Ananias and Saphira, as related by the author of the Acts.

In agreement with his wife, Saphira, Ananias had sold a property and kept back part of the proceeds of the sale. Bringing the remainder, he laid it at the Apostles' feet. Whereupon Peter said: "Ananias, how is it that Satan has taken possession of thy heart, bidding thee defraud the Holy Spirit by keeping back some of the money that was paid for the land?" Confounded, Ananias was overcome with terror and fell down dead.

Who does not remember Jesus' Last Supper with His disciples, when He who was about to die answered the disciple who asked Him about His betrayer: "Lord, who is it?" with the words: "It is the man to whom I give this piece of bread which I am dipping in the dish." Then He dipped the bread and gave it to Judas Iscariot, the son of Simon. The morsel once given, Satan entered into him [John 13:24-27].

In the parable of the sower, it is still Satan who comes in to steal away the good seed. The seed, Jesus explains to His disciples (accompanied, as St. Luke tells us, by certain women, whom He had freed from sicknesses, and Mary Magdalen, who had had seven devils cast out of her), is the word of God. Those by the wayside hear the word, and then the devil comes and takes it away from their hearts, so that they cannot find faith and be saved [Luke 8:1, 11-12].

The fact is that, while the legions of the demons are composed, it would seem, of rather primitive creatures, Satan himself exerts an influence that is cunning and all the more baneful in that it creeps into a man's mind almost without his knowledge. As St. John says in his Gospel, Satan is "the prince of this world" [John 12:31]. "This world" is wickedness, that is, the totality of the forces opposed to man's aspiration after God, to the growth of his spirituality, to his fight against the weaknesses of the flesh and, in general, against sin.

Sickness and Demoniacal Possession

In an age when the notion of sickness, such as we can now conceive it, was extremely vague and almost nonexistent, it is most remarkable to observe how strongly the Synoptists emphasize the distinction that Jesus maintained between the sick and the possessed. No doubt He considered that the demon was capable of producing the symptoms of diseases such as epilepsy, for example, but His attitude and practice toward the sick on the one hand and the possessed on the other are quite distinct. Full of pity and tenderness for the really sick and their friends, Jesus shows Himself to be full of tenderness, certainly, but reserved and severe toward the possessed. He touches the former, but seems much more discreet with the latter. He sets them free, but as if to say: "Yes, you are freed, but do not go back."

Whatever interpretation may be suggested of the actions of Jesus toward the sick and the possessed, one fact is clear: our Lord always distinguishes the one from the other by applying a different spiritual "medication" to each. On the sick He lays his hands, He touches them, anoints them gently with His saliva; to the others He administers an exorcism. And it is this exorcism which He hands on to His disciples and which they too will administer, wherever their apostolate may extend in the whole world.

True or False Possession?

Can we go further in the interpretation that the modern doctor may make of Jesus' message, relying only on the Gospel evidence? The doctor as such cannot claim the right to exceed the limits of his science, but as a sincere seeker he may well expound the teaching of qualified theologians.

For this reason the analysis propounded by Mgr. Catherinet in an article on "Demoniacs in the Gospel"[5] throws a vivid light on the theological concept of demoniacal possession. There can be no doubt, this author writes, that if the doctor confines his attention to the morbid symptoms, he will see in the woman bent double a paralytic, in the energumen of Gerasa a wild madman, in the boy cured on the morrow of the Transfiguration an epileptic. Each case of possession certainly seems to correspond to some bodily infirmity: the demon makes a man dumb, or deaf and dumb, or a lunatic; the evil spirit provokes convulsionary seizures. Now, all these undoubtedly pathological phenomena correspond to varying degrees of disturbance of the nervous system. Hence it follows that the neurologist is tempted to conclude that the possession is identical with a more or less precisely defined neurological or psychiatric disorder.

Can we then explain this singular fact that "diabolical possession is always accompanied, in the Gospel narratives, with clinical signs characteristic of an abnormal state of the nervous system"? According to Mgr. Catherinet, theologians place the activity of the devil at the intersection of the soul and the body. Thus the evil spirit can, with God's permission, profit by the

[5] F. M. Catherinet, "Les Démoniaques dans l'Évangile," in *Satan* (Paris: Desclée, 1948). English translation: "Demoniacs in the Gospel," in *Satan* (London and New York: Sheed and Ward, 1951), 163-177.

disorder which an already existing mental sickness may have introduced into the human composite, in order to provoke and enlarge a functional disorder, under cover of which it insinuates itself and makes its abode in the patient. From this theory it follows that, according to Catholic theology, every genuine diabolical possession is accompanied in fact and almost inevitably by mental and nervous disturbances, amplified by the influence of the "evil spirit" and sometimes created by it.

The doctor who wishes to remain a completely honest man cannot, then, a priori exclude the possibility of a transcendent causation in the production of certain neuropsychiatric disorders, whose natural source is not known to the expert.

Following this reasoning, we are convinced that to arrive at a sound judgment one should rely less on the external appearance of the possession and much more on apprehending the subtle and hidden springs set in motion in the profound and unique disturbances of the state of demoniacal possession.

These facts being granted, can we discover any more substantial teaching among the greatest masters of Christian religious psychology?

No one who has read and absorbed the doctrine of a St. John of the Cross or a St. Teresa of Jesus can possibly doubt it. Certainly the wonderful author of the *Foundations* and the *Relations* seems to have been really haunted by visible representations of the devil, for St. Teresa of Avila[6] depicts the evil one as possessing a hideous form, with a terrifying mouth, and as a regular Proteus, able to transform and multiply himself. It would be a mistake, however, to believe in the existence of authentic hallucinatory visions. St. Teresa herself says: "He rarely

---

[6] *Life*, ch. 28 (English edition, Penguin Books, 1957, chap. 22).

presented himself under a sensible form, but very often without any, as in that kind of vision where, without seeing any form, one sees someone to be present."[7]

What this great mystic perceived, then, was not so much a form as the feeling that a being was present: God or the devil. On a true view of the case one easily finds a connection of causality between the devil and those stubborn and perverse impulses of the inner life which are his best allies. We find the devil ensconced at the root of our errors, our illusions, our pride. Woe to the soul that hypnotizes itself with its own failings, that nurses some culpable habit! Disguised, cunning, insidious, and perverse, the devil advances only slowly and often under a guise that in itself has nothing wrong about it. Yet under this covering of benevolence is hidden an influence pernicious to the soul, causing it dereliction, sadness, and confusion.

It would no doubt be going too far to maintain that St. Teresa, long before Baudelaire, had understood that the devil's greatest cunning is to allow men to doubt his existence, but if that idea was not completely worked out, it was clearly experienced by her penetrating intuition.

According to St. John of the Cross, whose profound intuition and vast comprehension of the mystical soul we have tried to expound elsewhere,[8] the most that the devil can effect is to simulate, to assume the appearance of the Being of God.[9] Powerless to convey the true impression of the divine, the devil will

---

[7] Marcel Lépée, "Sainte-Thérèse de Jésus et le démon," in *Satan*, 98; English trans., 97-102.

[8] Jean Lhermitte, *Mystiques et faux mystiques* (Paris: Bloud et Gay, 1953).

[9] Lucien-Marie de Saint-Joseph, in *Satan*, 86, 97; English trans., 841-896.

make use of his favorite weapon, suggestion, to prevent the believer from giving his complete, total adherence to the Eternal. "To deprive a soul of God, to halt it on the way of union under any kind of pretext, to keep it in the relative when it is called to the Absolute, to dupe it by an appearance even of piety in order to distract it from the reality of God; that is what the devil aims at and what the soul must beware of from him." According to the great mystical Doctor, Satan cannot touch the soul once it has severed the bonds that attach it to the material world. "When the gates of the senses have been shut and the mystic plunges into the Night of the Senses in order to cleave more closely to God, the devil cannot touch him, for he cannot even know what is now happening in the soul."

The author of the *Ascent of Mount Carmel* is warning us against the danger of accepting external visions, internal representations, emotions, all that mechanism of the perceptible, in fact, which to one of goodwill may appear to be the means of reaching the highest peaks of the religious life, whereas in fact it diverts us from them.

When the soul desires the return of these sensible impressions, "it becomes very obstinate" and pride takes the place of humility, so that the mind embarks on a road which is more and more dangerous and from which it is hard to divert it. "The soul that is pure, cautious, simple and humble must resist revelations and other visions with as much effort and care as though they were very perilous temptations."[10]

The devil is indeed "God's ape," and the better to oppose God's work in the soul, he begins by counterfeiting that work

[10]St. John of the Cross, *Ascent of Mount Carmel*, trans. Allison Peers (London, 1943), bk. 2, ch. 27.

by artifice. And so, according to the teaching of St. John of the Cross, the devil is far less to be feared in so-called external manifestations than in the underground influence he exerts in souls that are not sufficiently instructed or well tempered.

Chapter 2

Paroxysmal Forms of
Pseudo-Diabolical Possession

Epileptic Attacks

The chief example of these forms, which has struck the imagination of many, corresponds to the "falling sickness," epilepsy. The violent convulsive seizure assumes such an impressive appearance that it is easy to understand how the earliest witnesses supposed that the patient must be invaded or possessed by some supernatural power, the devil. What happens is that during these cataclysmic states the patient loses consciousness, his personality seems to be completely superseded, driven out, ravished, for he abandons himself to actions that seem beyond the powers of a normal person. The strength he exerts during the attack seems to exceed his natural endowment.

Another misleading feature is that, once the convulsive crisis has passed, the patient displays a strange psychological "postictal" state when, in the hidden depths of consciousness, the mind gives free rein to divagations, sometimes bearing on a religious theme. In other cases, if the patient does not express his anguish in words, it is unmistakably depicted on his face.

For instance, Patrikios (of Athens) observed a patient whose features in the course of the attack expressed a profoundly distressed moral state: after recovering his senses he replied: "I cannot exactly describe the sights I have just seen, but it was fearful," and he buried his face in his hands.

I should add that if the psychological aura (the premonitory phenomenon of the seizure) appears in some common cases which are filled with feelings or representations of a supernatural type, it may sometimes be falsely attributed by the patient to the invasion of a demoniacal power. But cases of this kind are in fact very rare, and the manifestations of epilepsy, on the other hand, involve signs and characteristics that barely permit of any error of judgment.[11]

It was not the same in the days of Briquet and Charcot, in whose works may still be found the description of paroxysmal convulsive attacks, called hystero-epileptic. While we should not deny the reality of these paroxysms, in which are combined two states different in nature, hysteria[12] and epilepsy, we may agree that facts of that sort deserve no more than a mention.

It is well known that one of the most distinctive marks of epilepsy is the dissolution of consciousness during the seizures. Nonetheless, no one now doubts that, in contrast with amnesiac epileptic seizures or attacks, there are psychomotor or purely psychological attacks that are not accompanied by the abolition of consciousness or memory. The patient is present

[11]Epileptic seizures can be confirmed with confidence by modern medical tests, most notably, an EEG (electroencephalogram). — Ed.

[12]Today called "conversion disorder." A conversion disorder involving seizure-like activity is often referred to as a "pseudo-seizure." — Ed.

like a spectator at strange phenomena, but he still regards them as pathological. We may be excused from dwelling further on their description, which is the business of the neurologist.

Psychoneuroses and Hysteria (Conversion Disorder)

So long as animism prevailed—"the greatest power given to men" said Napoleon, "is to give a soul to things which have none"—it was not surprising that epileptics were thought to be possessed: the brutal transformation of their behavior, their complete unconsciousness, seemed to be incontrovertible evidence. But when epilepsy had become clearly identified, the attention of doctors and exorcists was directed to another type of convulsionaries.

While the epileptic attack is confined to the individual, there are other demonopathic attacks which are marked by their influence on, and extension to, those around. History records numerous epidemics of convulsionaries, which abounded more particularly in the fifteenth, sixteenth, and seventeenth centuries.

In these cases, the external transformation of the physical and moral personality gives the patient a much closer resemblance to what one might imagine a genuine possession to be, for not only is the sufferer's body affected with convulsions and contractures of extraordinary force, assuming attitudes which are lewd, grotesque, or theatrical, but the subject indulges in vulgarities, obscenities, insulting and blasphemous invective, shouting that it is the devil or devils which possess him and are acting in him.

Unlike the epileptic paroxysm, which is short and ends with a period of unconsciousness or sleep, these demonopathic attacks may sometimes go on for very long periods, even for hours. Facts of this kind have given rise to the term *demono-pathic hysterical madness.*

The word *madness*, now almost meaningless in psychiatry and neurology, is of course open to objection, but what is not so (for examples have been, and are, very numerous) is the reality of a very special mental state, with a pattern of paroxysmal crises or attacks, characterized by an apparent transformation of the personality, which shows itself in a great disorder of attitude, actions, and behavior, combined with a feeling of being possessed by the unclean spirit: the evil one, the devil.

The religious history of France presents numerous cases of this type of demonopathic hysteria, which is by no means extinct. We select one example, that of Marie-Thérèse Noblet.

Marie-Thérèse Noblet

Was Marie-Thérèse Noblet a case of hysteria, asks P. Giscard, or a mystic? We may remark, in the first place, that the former hypothesis does not exclude the latter and that some very genuine mystics have been affected by nervous troubles of a hysterical nature. Françoise Minkowska has rightly insisted on the need to substitute *and* for *or* if we are to assess the facts correctly.

Thanks to the well-documented book by Fr. Pineau,[13] we have accurate knowledge of the remarkable events in the checkered career of this servant of the Lord in Papua, and in the *Études Carmélitaines*[14] will be found appreciations of her by a psychiatrist, a psychologist, and a neurologist.

[13] André Pineau, *Marie-Thérèse Noblet, servante du Seigneur en Papouasie* (Paris: P. Dillen, 1934).
[14] *La nuit mystique* (October 1938) and *Le risque chrétien* (April 1939).

Paroxysmal Forms of Pseudo-Diabolical Possession

As Roland Dalbiez emphasized, Marie-Thérèse appears first of all as a frequent beneficiary of sudden cures. She was cured of acute peritonitis at the age of seven; at thirteen, of spinal pains accompanied by various nervous troubles; then of cardiac arrhythmia, a quinsied cough, and paralysis of the legs and the left arm, which induced Dr. Chipault to diagnose not Pott's disease but, more cautiously, "a localized vertebral lesion, complicated by a general nervous condition."[15] At twenty-one she had appendicitis and the same sudden cure. At twenty-four, fever and vomitings, the nature of which is still mysterious; ten years later, complete blindness, which likewise disappeared. Marie-Thérèse in fact displayed a whole series of maladies that, we are told, "sometimes brought her to the edge of the grave." After her arrival in Papua she was made dumb for two years by the demon.

We have not yet done with her symptoms, always strange and rapidly curable: palpitations, thoracic pains, paralysis of the left arm and leg, followed by apparently miraculous cures.

Even before her departure for Papua, Marie-Thérèse said she was the victim of pestering and annoyance by the demon. One day, for example, the evil one ransacked and broke everything it found in her room; more, it tied her by the hairs of her head to the bedrails. The demon often appeared to her and practiced the utmost cruelties on the unfortunate girl. During an exorcism, she saw the demon at her feet, had it beaten, and put her foot on its head. Another time the evil one "caught her up from the couch on which she was resting, and threw her violently on to her bed, saying: 'Ah! that's how you obey!'" Then in a

[15] As in the cases of pseudo-Pott's disease, which are numerous, no radiography, no examination of the cerebrospinal fluid, or even a neurological examination had been carried out.

relentless grip it carried her off into Hell, and tormented her with the sight of the damned, the devils and beasts. The demon also took the form of animals. During her voyage from France to Papua, she once saw a gorilla on the bridge and was surprised that those with her saw nothing. Of course, this gorilla did not hesitate to attack her on the following days, to beat her, then to inflict on her a "triple attack." During the night, she said, she was also visited by the evil one, which sometimes took a human form, "for instance, lifting the mosquito net of one of her little sisters. She went to it and in a low voice ordered it in the name of God to depart. It obeyed, but instead of going down the stairs, it entered the room, threw itself upon her and covered her with blows." Having invoked the holy angels she fainted, and when she came to herself she found herself still on the floor, her gown pulled on, a pillow under her head, her woolen cover over and under her, and her room filled with the scent of eau de cologne. When she wrote to her exorcist, "the demon snatched away the letter, crumpled it and tore it up." She was again attacked by devils in the form of a monkey and two dogs. One night when she had gone down with two sisters to chase three horses out of the compound, a fourth horse with flashing eyes dashed violently upon her without her seeing it coming, knocked her over, and kicked her—a horse "unknown in the district."

Another night, Satan threw her to the foot of the bed and beat her cruelly; he dragged her by her hair into the dormitory, then into her room, a knee on her chest; he tried repeatedly, but in vain, "to make her promise obedience to him, Satan." Two days later, there was "torture by three diabolic harpies." Always, during the night, she saw shadows creeping past the beds of the Papuan sisters. Near the bed of a sister, she seized an arm, but the brute struck her and covered her with blows. "While she was stretched on the ground, one Kanaka pulled her arms, another her feet … a third breathed out his foul breath in torrents of words; and gripping her throat, the devil, in the form of the supposed Kanaka, threatened to strangle her and clawed at her breast." The devil again urged her to say or do mad things.

The forms it took were innumerable: sometimes a gorilla, sometimes a horse with flashing eyes, now a shadow, now a human form, now a dog, sometimes even a creature of light. "Surrounded by its minions, it was of terrible beauty, but its eyes were full of hate."

Without doubt, all these stories are extraordinary enough, not to say extravagant, but there was worse to follow. Lucifer carried her off into infamous places, attacking her will by suggestions, images, and words. Another time, having carried her again into an evil place, "the devil showed her a soul very dear to her, taking part in horrors and blasphemies and sacrilegious mockeries against the vows of religion."

From time to time there were phenomena of movement: violent shakings of the torso or blows of the fist on the back, to the bewilderment of the bystanders. It was the same with the noises, the uproar, the commotion that went on in the house and even on the roofs. "One evening at La Gineste," reports Fr. Desna, "Monseigneur was performing the exorcisms, I believe, at the sisters' house. I was in the opposite room with Br. Paul. Suddenly we heard an infernal din on the stairway. At the same time, gigantic blows of a mallet seemed to fall against the walls."

As we have already seen, the devil can, if he likes, assume a human shape. But in some cases the cloven hoof appears, as we may judge from the following episode, which the exorcist calls the "officer-devil." In her youth Marie-Thérèse had indulged a

sentimental attachment for a brilliant officer who greatly ad-
mired her and wished to marry her. She refused, in order to keep
herself entirely for God. But one day the devil, who according
to Leon Bloy is always "a terrible gallant," disguised himself in
the likeness of this officer. "In full military uniform he presented
himself at La Gineste and asked to see Marie-Thérèse in the
drawing room." She ran there and stayed for a short while.

The exorcist was then at his desk, when he saw her come
in, with pale face and fast beating heart. Unable to speak, she
pointed to the drawing room. The exorcist at once went in; not
a soul was there, but the air was filled with a cloud of yellow
smoke, rising slowly to the ceiling. Great astonishment: then
she told him how she had just escaped from a dangerous attempt
of the devil, in the shape of her former lover; the devil had, in
fact, "tried to touch her heart through her regret for lost love"
and urged her to marry him. When she refused his advances the
demon-lover became brutal and threatened to carry her off by
force. By this violence Marie-Thérèse recognized him and with
the help of her guardian angel she succeeded in escaping him.

Here are stories indeed of which the least we can say is that
they are very strange, even allowing for their setting in Papua,
where sorcery is common. But the devil does not stick at appearances, blows, or bruises; if we are to believe P. Giscard and
Ch. Grimbert, the evil spirit demonstrated his existence by ir-
refutable facts.

Thus one day when Marie-Thérèse was ill, they brought her
a little wine, which she poured into a wineglass. As soon as she
had drunk it, she was seized with a violent quinsied cough, at
the same time feeling pricks in her throat. The nurse looked
at the bottom of the glass, and there she saw four pins. A pin
swallowed by Marie-Thérèse passed through her organs and

eventually lodged in her left side and was evacuated only seven months later, on August 15. Exorcised some days after this incident, the devil answered by the girl's mouth that he had obtained the pins in the house of a certain Tambon, a surveyor, living at Château Gombert.

Another time Marie-Thérèse was the victim of terrible heart attacks. The priest who came to see her prepared a glass of water on a tray, pouring in some drops of peppermint. He covered up the glass to protect it. But in the middle of the night the patient wanted to drink. At the first sip she stopped; the water had changed to ink.

I must quote one more event: the tying up at La Betheline. On January 18, 1917, with consummate art the devil bound her tightly with a strong cord, wound it around her from head to foot, in tight coils, and threw her on his back to carry her off. While this was going on the devoted nurse came in unexpectedly, but already the devil had hastily dropped his burden and disappeared. Fr. Jullien was called at once and found the poor girl all bruised and tied up like a parcel. He even states that it was too complicated to untie the skillful, tight knots; the bonds had to be carefully cut. "I can state," wrote the nurse, "that we had no rope in the room and that it was quite impossible for Marie-Thérèse to tie herself up in that way. Besides, I was there all the time, *in the next room.*"

If I have devoted so much space to stories of the wonders worked by Satan in his cruelty against a poor innocent missionary sister, it is because these demoniacal assaults were reported with the utmost seriousness and are credited not only by the blindly credulous but by certain doctors. In proof of the reality of the diabolical possession they quote the tying up of Marie-Thérèse's body by the "evil spirit," as well as the episode of the glass of peppermint changed into ink and the introduction of pins into a glass of wine. "The details matter little," writes Ch. Grimbert. "What is important is that such events were associated with a well-established simplicity of attitude."

But unfortunately we are no longer in the days of Jacob of Voragine![16] Everyone knows that the conjurer's commonest trick is to tie himself in knots, and the tricks of changing peppermint-water into ink or of introducing pins into a wineglass are even simpler. One still hears of masochists who for their own peculiar ends tie their bodies up with ropes or even iron chains, so that it is difficult to release them. I have personal experience of such cases. I may add that the devil's binding the "possessed" to some part of her bed has historical precedent. Magdalen of the Cross, the "diabolical abbess," is one example. This notorious prioress of the Poor Clares of Cordova was another who impressed all around her, even more than did Marie-Thérèse, by her air of recollection, her piety, her strict observance of the rule, so that she was considered a saint even in her lifetime.

If there are still any who can think that the introduction of pins into a glass of wine or the tying up of one's own body are marvels, they must be sadly ignorant of the tricks and illusions of conjurers! To an "illusionist" these spells attributed to Satan are child's play.[17]

---

[16] Bl. Jacob of Voragine (c. 1230-1298), bishop of Genoa and author of the *Golden Legend*, a collection of lives of medieval saints that was popular in the Middle Ages.

[17] But the inclination to believe in the mysterious, in magic, is such that even now the conjurer is sometimes taken for a clairvoyant, a being with supernatural powers. A famous conjurer told me that one day, before a gathering of educated people, after showing some new tricks, he had declared: "Now

Paroxysmal Forms of Pseudo-Diabolical Possession

As far as one can judge from the brief but accurate analysis of the diabolical manifestations in connection with Marie-Thérèse Noblet, they were always produced at intervals, usually at night and always in the absence of any observer. Nobody could ever see the strange demon, whether as gorilla, dog, Kanaka, ordinary man or brilliant cavalryman, and with good reason.

But if this Satan, so often invoked by our heroine, hopelessly evades our grasp, can we discover in her conduct any signs that may lead to the discovery of the source of these strange and often very disconcerting phenomena?

Fr. Pineau's book, which may be taken as very accurate, helps to resolve our doubts. There we read, in fact, that Marie-Thérèse underwent very many exorcisms, during which demoniacal possession was manifested either completely or incompletely. In the former case consciousness disappeared; in the latter, the possessed could follow the exorcisms. The crisis showed itself first, we are told, by a general rigidity of the body, which the exorcist had to break down; when the rigid seizure had softened, her rage (as one possessed) and her (apparent) suffering began to increase. Her limbs and body shuddered or flinched as if they were physically afflicted by the punishments invoked on the devil.

---

then, I am going to show you how I work these tricks." "No!" someone replied. "There is something else to it."

Another friend of mine who amused himself with "thought-reading" told me a similar story. After a session of so-called revelations and clairvoyance, having avowed that it was all tricks and inventions, he was met with the retort: "No, you may not know it, but you are certainly a clairvoyant." I remember that a book was written in the eighteenth century to prove that conjurers were the devil's magicians.

"She became rigid gradually. She threw away everything she had, the blessed objects far away. Her face changed, I did not recognize her: I was afraid of her."

"What movements did she make?"

"She had jerky movements. At first, she became rigid in great spasms. Gradually her limbs became rigid as iron. Her head was turned backwards in a terrifying way. Her limbs were rigid and gripped by terrible spasms."

"She lost consciousness and was struck down as by an electric current," wrote Mlle. Polle, who was present. She lost consciousness; her limbs rigid, she was shaken with convulsions. Although the patient seemed to be suffering some profound pain, it was noticed that her body was insensible. The demonopathic attack had already lasted from a half to three-quarters of an hour from the beginning.

Questioned on the phenomenon of the contractures, the exorcist answered that "the initial rigidity of the attack was most frequent at Marseilles; that then the head was reversed, the features hard, angular, unrecognizable. The arc of a circle made by her body gave the impression that only the heels and the occiput rested on the ground."

Is not this a most realistic account of the demonopathic attack of hysterical patients, a description exactly modeled on that which we owe to Charcot, Paul Richer, and Gilles de la Tourette? It is an attack that all the neurologists— attentive and conscientious observers—have often observed, but unlike others they have not been duped by it.

On this point a story told by Fr. Eschimann is instructive :

Coming down the mountains to visit Kubuna, I found Marie-Thérèse ill at the infirmary. I found her tired, but normal, smiling as usual. After asking for all sorts of news about up-country, Marie-Thérèse was suddenly seized with violent convulsions … her eyes haggard, her body bent in a bow, raised up, her hands clutching nervously. Suspecting nothing, I concluded she must be in the last throes of the death-agony. I rose to call for help, but after half a minute her body fell back on the bed. Marie-Thérèse, now calm, opened her eyes, looked at me and said: "But, M. Eschimann, weren't you afraid?" "Me, afraid? Afraid of what?" [And he concludes:] I never suspected any diabolical or other business, in this case of convulsion—so long as Marie-Thérèse lived.

I shall have to return later to this state of consciousness during the major attacks: in the case of what may be called the minor attacks, it is hard to deny that she retained contact with the world about her. Also, these "lucid dialogues" correspond with those of which we read in bygone days.

Like Sr. Jeanne of the Angels, prioress of the Ursulines of Loudun, Marie-Thérèse was subjected to an enormous number of exorcisms, with the object of rescuing her from the power of the "evil spirit," while the exorcist never suspected that such practices only aggravated the passions of the so-called "possessed" person.

As Abbé Bremond remarks about Fr. Surin: "The exorcist too easily accepted the weird notion of the exorcist's role held by a good many theologians, not heeding the disastrous results entailed by such a gross disregard of the letter and spirit of the Roman Ritual."

Through Marie-Thérèse's mouth, the devil expressed ideas wholly opposed to religion, uttered foul blasphemies, at the same time exciting his victim's body and making it wildly agitated. Let this example suffice :

> The exorcist placed his episcopal cross on Marie-Thérèse's mouth and said: "You shall kiss it, the cross of Christ." "No, not that!" "Yes, foul beast, you shall kiss it." "Never!" "You shall kiss it, the cross of your Master.... Leave this child of God: she is his own daughter." "I want her." "You shall not have her." "I want her to be mine." "You shall never have her; she belongs to us, she is God's. Leave her, foul beast, I scorn you!" "If you scorn me, I detest you." "So much the better." "You are nothing." "Well I know it, but I have the power of my priesthood to torment you with, and I shall not spare you."

I repeat: I have tried to give an analysis of Marie-Thérèse Noblet's case simply on account of the problems posed by such a case for the consciences of the doctor and the theologian.

Sr. Jeanne of the Angels

History is indeed full of events that have been given the label of "diabolical possession," such as the case of Marie-Thérèse Noblet, and too many names come to mind for us to record them all here. But the most illuminating of them all, perhaps, is that of the notorious Sr. Jeanne of the Angels, prioress of the Ursuline convent at Loudun, whose memorable story is linked with that of Fr. Surin.[18]

Somewhat unruly as a child, and of a caustic temperament, Mlle. de Berciel, who at the age of twenty-five was to become

---

[18]Henri Bremond, *Histoire littéraire du sentiment religieux en France*, Vol. 5, *La conquête mystique*.

Sr. Jeanne of the Angels, presents a picture very similar to the one we have been describing, except that in her case eroticism was plainly apparent, while in Marie-Thérèse it can only be suspected. But in either case the influence of the exorcisms, constantly repeated in defiance of the prescriptions of the Roman Ritual, was disastrous.

It may seem surprising that she should have been so quickly entrusted with the office of prioress; but although her deformed physique was not attractive of sympathy, her intelligence, her name, and her culture were bound to attract attention. Exerting an influence about her which was all the more formidable because well disguised, the mother prioress was the victim of illusions, and perhaps of feigned apparitions during the night. Draped phantoms glided between the dormitory beds, snatched off the coverings, touched faces with icy fingers. In the minds of the exorcists of that age, all this bogus supernatural could only be diabolical.

Like Marie-Thérèse, Sr. Jeanne was the object of diabolical visits and spiteful vexations; like her, she saw near her men with a foul stench: "They seized her with great fury by the arms, they stripped her and fastened her to the bed-post."

Things got to the point when the exorcisms were performed, no longer behind closed doors, but in public. And so one day the door of the Ursuline convent was opened and after a third exorcism the mother superior was taken with convulsions: "violences, vexations, howlings, and grindings of teeth," which left the poor woman exhausted.

But already other nuns besides her seemed to be possessed and afflicted with the same malady. Sometimes, M. de Nion informs us, they passed their left foot over their shoulders to their cheeks. They also raised their feet up to their heads, until their big toes touched the nose. Others again were able to stretch their legs so far to the left and right that they sat on the ground, without any space being visible between their bodies and the floor. One, the mother superior, stretched her legs to such an extraordinary extent that, from toe to toe, the distance was seven feet, though she herself was but four feet high. The remarkable thing, which surprised the observers, was that in spite of the intensity and frequency of the convulsive attacks, which were thought to be diabolical assaults, the health of the possessed nuns appeared to be in no way affected: those who were somewhat delicate seemed healthier than before the possession.

As with Marie-Thérèse, what gave color to the theory of demoniacal possession was not only the display of strength and the vigor of the subjects during the attacks, but rather the apparent change in their personalities. How, it was said, could one account for the nuns' being capable of gestures and attitudes so opposed to decency and even, it seemed, so beyond physical strength, without admitting the intervention of some occult supernatural power which, since it could not be divine, must be demoniacal? This belief was strengthened by what the prioress herself said about her state.

One must always, of course, be very skeptical about anything to do with the confessions of hysterical subjects, who are often without any sense of reality and truth, but we should not reject them out of hand.

Now, according to Sr. Jeanne, her mind, during the attacks, seemed not only darkened but more and more confused until, finally, consciousness disappeared. When she recovered her senses, she said, she had no recollection of what had been said and done by those around her. We shall return later to the problem of defining the state of consciousness during hysterical attacks.

But the evidence for Sr. Jeanne was there: could she who had shown such signs of intelligence and piety that she had been raised to the highest post in the Ursuline community abandon herself, while fully conscious of her actions, to behavior so coarse and so crudely opposed to the most elementary decency?

Fr. Surin set to work on the prioress, writes Killigrew, a cruel but perceptive observer. After a few minutes of the exorcism the demon Balaam made his appearance. There were writhings and convulsions. Sr. Jeanne's belly suddenly swelled, until it looked like that of a woman far gone in pregnancy; then the breasts puffed themselves up to the size of the belly. The exorcist applied relics to each part as it was affected, and the swellings subsided. Killigrew touched her hand: it was cool. He felt her pulse: it was calm and slow. The prioress pushed him aside and began to claw at her coif. A moment later the bald, close-shaven head was bare. She rolled up her eyes, she stuck out her tongue. It was prodigiously swollen, black in color, and had the pimply texture of Morocco leather.

Surin now untied her, ordering Balaam to adore the Blessed Sacrament. Sr. Jeanne slid backward off her seat and landed on the floor.

Then as she lay on her back, she bent her waist like a tumbler and went so, shoving herself with her heels, on her bare shaven head, all about the chapel after the friar. And many other strange, unnatural postures, beyond anything that ever I saw, or could believe possible for any man or woman to do. Nor was this a sudden motion, and away: but a continuous thing, which she did for above an hour together; and yet not out of breath nor hot with all the motions used.[19]

Throughout the whole attack the prioress had not uttered a word, but suddenly she gave a piercing cry and spoke the word: "Joseph!" This was the sign, the mark, they all cried, which the devil had promised to make when it went out. And in fact there could be seen on Sr. Jeanne's forearm a ruddy color rising, about an inch long, and in it many red specks, representing the word *Joseph*. To this supposed graphic stigma, which the prioress exhibited to so many sightseers at the court, to the cardinal duke, to the king and the queen, were soon added the names of Jesus, Mary, and St. Francis de Sales.

We may read in Bremond[20] the whole development of this weird story, which strikes us as a burlesque, arousing naive credulity in some, skepticism in others. For while most of those who visited Sr. Jeanne had no doubt that the phenomena were supernatural, some remained extremely skeptical, wondering whether these impressive demonstrations concealed some fraudulent or deceptive device, and all the more because they knew by direct experience how demons ought to be expelled: with the whip. As Aldous Huxley surmises: "In many cases old-fashioned whipping was probably just as effective as modern shock-treatment."

Well known, too, were all the criteria the Church holds to be decisive of genuine possession, but they were scarcely

---

[19] Quoted in Aldous Huxley, *The Devils of Loudun* (London: Chatto and Windus, 1952), pp. 291-292.

[20] Bremond, *Histoire littéraire du sentiment religieux en France.*

heeded. Thus, on November 24, 1632, in the presence of M. de Cerisay, the exorcist proffered the sacred host to one of the five demons—Asmodeus, Leviathan, Balaam, Behemoth, and Isacaaron—by whom Sr. Jeanne claimed to be possessed, saying: *Quem adoras?* ["Whom do you adore?"], to which she replied: *Jesus Christus*. "This devil is not up to it," remarked one of the bystanders. The exorcist, changing the form of his question, asked: *Quis est iste quem adoras?* ["Who is it that you adore?"], receiving the reply: *Jesu Christe*. Of all the demons present, not one was a moderate Latinist!

As we have observed, according to all those who have striven to define the mental state of hysterical patients—and Charcot, in every one of his lectures, insisted strongly on this—it is very difficult, in the accounts given by these subjects, to discern the false from the true, illusion from fact. Not that illusion can always be taken for pretense, for voluntary lying; this may derive from a disturbance of judgment, a retreat of the mind into the state of childhood, which is known for its aptitude to create myths and inventions, void of foundation and perfectly disinterested.[21]

Although one must decline to accept Sr. Jeanne's sayings too readily, one should not neglect them; one may even interpret them. In the autobiography she wrote many years after the

---

[21] With hysteria cases, of course, some practical end often lies at the root of their behavior, but it is doubtful whether these patients have a clear idea of it. As E. Dupré has well said, mythomania must not be confused with lying: the former is pathological in nature and is connected with the bodily mythoplasticity in the hysterical subject, while the latter is a type of behavior and action deliberately consented to, and based on reasons of interest, especially of vanity.

events we have described, the mother superior thus analyzes the state of her mind:

> I did not then believe that one could be possessed with-
> out having given consent to, or made a pact with, the
> devil; in which I was mistaken.... I myself was not of the
> number of the innocent, for thousands and thousands of
> times I had given myself over to the devil by commit-
> ting sin.... The demons insinuated themselves into my
> mind and inclinations, in such sort that, through the evil
> dispositions they found in me, they made of me one and
> the same substance with themselves.... Ordinarily they
> acted in conformity with the feelings I had in my soul;
> this they did so subtly that I myself did not believe that I
> had any demons within me.

It must, therefore, have been under the pressure of the exorcists that Sr. Jeanne and her companions thought themselves
to be possessed and behaved as such.

I would make it clear that at certain times Sr. Jeanne presented the clinical picture that in her time was supposed to
be that of diabolical possession, without being completely the
dupe of this so-called possession. Moreover, she felt herself able
to guide or bridle one or other of the seven demons that inhab-
ited her personality, letting herself believe that this was a mark
of sanctification. But during the great paroxysms of fury that
occurred in public, it seems that we must accept her statement
as true and agree that there was a temporary but genuine alien-
ation of self-awareness.

On this subject I think I should repeat the admission made
to me, many years ago, by one of my patients, a foreigner. When
I asked if he had ever had syphilis, he replied: "Why, of course,

in my country most of the men are syphilitics and hysterical." This revelation on the part of a man of high intelligence surprised me greatly, so I questioned him as to how his consciousness was affected during the severe attacks of hysteria he had frequently experienced. "At first," he replied, "one's consciousness is clear, and one is sure that the will is going to be strong enough to check the onset of the symptoms, but very soon one is carried away in a wild automatism. One knows no more; contact is lost."

All the same, while the suspension of consciousness and memory is very real, it does not go so deep as that caused by epilepsy.

Marthe Brossier

In his important work on Mme. Acarie (Bl. Mary of the Incarnation), in which I had a small share, Fr. Bruno de Jésus-Marie recounts the strange story of a girl of Romorantin, called Marthe Brossier.[22] It all took place in 1599, a year after Henri IV's promulgation of the Edict of Nantes, which troubled the consciences of certain Catholics; an attempt was made to obtain the repeal of the edict. At the opportune moment, a so-called possessed person was discovered, who declaimed "through her devil" against the Huguenots. "She spoke marvelous things against the Huguenots, and her devil went about every day to find some new soul to put in its cauldron, saying that all the Huguenots belonged to it. And in Paris whoever did not believe it, and doubted that Marthe was really possessed by the devil, was judged a heretic."

[22]Bruno de J. M., O.C.D., *La Belle Acarie* (Paris: Desclée de Brouwer, 1942).

True or False Possession?

Marthe's transports, trances, and convulsive paroxysms were of the same stuff as we have seen at Loudun. Jacques Le Prévost wrote to Bérulle: "Beelzebub puffed out her belly, then bent her body back till her head touched her feet from behind, often crying out, 'I am worse tormented than if I were in Hell.'"

Believing that it was no case of genuine possession, but more simply some grave mental disorder, Henri IV had Marthe confined in the Grand Châtelet, where she was kindly treated. After a long examination by the doctors, who drew up detailed reports, Marthe was sent on an order of the Parlement to her father at Romorantin and placed under the supervision of a magistrate. No wiser plan could have been devised. But to reassure public opinion, too prone to see every case of convulsions as proof of diabolical possession, Henri IV caused a report on her case to be published in May 1599. It was written by the physician Marescot and is a model of analysis and perspicacity.

I reproduce what I said about it in a note to the text of Fr. Bruno's *La Belle Acarie*.[23]

Appearing before a commission of chosen doctors and in presence of the ecclesiastical authority, Marthe Brossier developed some symptoms which were apparently very singular. For instance, she claimed to understand Latin and Greek. But questioned by Marescot and the bishop, both in Latin and in Greek, she answered nothing.

Conducted to the chapel, Marthe knelt ... immediately fell into a reverie, resting first on her buttocks, then

[23] Bruno de J. M., O.C.D., *La Belle Acarie*, 439 ff. For an account in English, based on Fr. Bruno's book and the available source material, see Lancelot C. Sheppard, *Barbe Acarie, Wife and Mystic* (New York: David McKay Co., 1953), 59-60.

on her back and shoulders, then gently on her head. Lying on her back, drawing deep breaths, her flanks heaving, like a horse after running, she rolled her eyes and put out her tongue.

The exorcisms being renewed the next day, "the said Marthe collapsed at certain words, recovered herself briskly, flouted the exorcists and made fun of them."

During another session, she again "put out her tongue, rolled her eyes at the sound of certain words: *Et homo factus est, Verbum taro factum est, Tantum ergo sacramentum*; she fell as before, shaking herself in the manner of convulsions."

Marescot, wishing to test the reality of these symptoms which had so intrigued the exorcists, gripped Marthe by the scruff of the neck, "ordering her to stand still." Unable to shake any longer, and seeing her imposture discovered, she said: "It has gone, it has left me." Previously, "Duret pricked her with a pin between thumb and forefinger," and Marthe seemed to feel no pain. The doctors, however, "having long deliberated together and considered all things they thought should be considered, reported to the bishop, by the consent of all and through the mouth of the said Marescot, their opinion, which in a few words was this: *Nihil a daemone, multa ficta, a morboso pauca* (Nothing from the demon, many things feigned, a few from the state of disease). Later on, "one of them stated that she had the devil in her body, because she put her tongue so far out and had endured the pinprick." But "the others firmly and constantly asserted for certain that all Marthe's actions were feigned and simulated, as had formerly been reported."

True or False Possession?

Marescot discusses what reasons can argue in favor of genuine demoniacal possession, for he is thoroughly convinced (the point is noteworthy) of the existence of a real power of the devil over certain persons. Starting from the fundamental principle that one should attribute to demoniacal influence only those phenomena which nature cannot produce unaided, he concludes that nothing in the facts he has been able to observe in Marthe Brossier can be classed as extra-natural and therefore demoniacal.

Does he include the convulsions? But these can be reproduced by tumblers and mountebanks. The limbs of genuine convulsionaries are so stiff that nobody can bend them; put a finger between their jaws and you risk being fast gripped and bitten. Now Marthe did nothing of this sort; in fact, she not only suspended her convulsive movements but stopped herself at the priest's command. And Marescot concludes that Marthe, so far from being possessed by a demon, should be considered an impostor.

To demonstrate the weakness of the arguments adduced in support of Marthe's possession, he considers one by one the so-called proofs on which they rely.

First, insensibility to the pricks. Certainly, Marthe appeared not to feel anything when her skin was pierced with a pin, and one cannot even doubt the fact that the pricks were not followed by any bleeding. But are these phenomena beyond nature, so that they cannot be explained by natural processes? No, replies our author. Many tumblers or mountebanks can pierce their skins with a needle without, apparently, feeling any pain. There is nothing strange in there being no bleeding from the wounded part, for in order to produce bleeding a small vein, at least, must be pierced. Pursuing his analysis of anesthesia,

Marescot observes that concentration on one point can reduce feelings to the point of suppressing them. The Stoics had long ago judged that if one is resolved not to feel, one feels nothing. Can one admit, finally, that the devil suspends one's sensation? The contrary can be more readily believed.

The author then returns, with a special emphasis which is not surprising, to the paroxysmal convulsions during which Marthe protruded her tongue, turned her head around, rolled her eyes up, heaved her flanks, gritted her teeth, and finally struggled convulsively. With genuine convulsionaries, Marescot observes, the attack produces extreme fatigue and the patients emerge from their paroxysm confused and bewildered. This was not the case with Marthe, who, when the attack was over, appeared quite natural, neither confused nor exhausted. During the convulsive attacks, Marthe heaved her flanks separately, but there is nothing extraordinary about that. Horses do the same to recover their breath.

As an even stranger symptom, certain doctors thought they observed that Marthe could "speak from the stomach" without opening her lips. As we should say now, she was a ventriloquist. But had not Hippocrates observed the same thing, without claiming to witness a phenomenon that could not be explained by a natural, physiological process?

As Marescot urges, it is possible that while keeping the mouth shut an articulate sound may cause the lining of the trachea to vibrate and give the illusion of a thoracic or abdominal voice. In any case, he says, he has never observed that Marthe gave the impression of being a ventriloquist.

It was claimed, he goes on, that Marthe proved herself able to understand Greek and Latin, having never studied these languages. Pure falsehood: Marthe had never spoken any but the language of her district, Romorantin. Had she not admitted, moreover, that she did not understand Latin? If she had answered the interrogating priest with some Latin phrases, this was because she had already heard them. Did Marthe's powers of perception and recognition reveal some special character, inexplicable by nature alone? Not at all. In fact, when she was offered holy water to drink, she noticed nothing, while she fell into a trance on being given ordinary water from a holy-water stoup. Again, she was easily deceived over relics. She had been presented with a key, wrapped up, and told that it was a fragment of the true Cross, upon which she began her "diableries," just as she went into violent convulsions when addressed with the well-known tag from Virgil, *Arma virumque cano*, thinking that it was from a book of exorcisms.

Much had been made, Marescot adds, of a phenomenon that was certainly inexplicable, if true: Marthe had been seen suspended in the air without support. But, he ironically observes, the judges had never seen this in the morning, but only in the afternoon, when fumes had obscured their brains and excited their imaginations!

Therefore, Marescot concludes, Marthe was neither possessed nor sick: all the phenomena she displayed were trickery. But then, with what object, *cui bono*, did this girl abandon herself to such extravagances? Did she deceive for the pleasure of deceiving?

Throughout this discussion, Marescot shows himself far in advance of his contemporaries, for we have to wait for Charcot and his school before the problem of morbid simulation is faced. We now know that there exists a category of persons who reveal an aptitude for lying, simulating, and cheating, and all with the sole aim, conscious or unconscious, of attracting attention. But,

Marescot continues, is there not some disguised motive of self-interest that, consciously or unconsciously, is urging Marthe to feign these "diableries"? And he notes that this self-styled "possessed" girl was perhaps not unprofitable to her father, who received sums of money toward his daughter's cure.

The last question he discusses is this: How could an uneducated girl like Marthe display such skill in "devilries"? The shrewd author remarks that she had read some books on "devilry" and also that several people had told her that "she had the devil in her."

As we can see, Marescot's aim is not merely to establish the reality of Marthe Brossier's deceit, but also to trace the origin of this disorder of the imagination to its source. Lies, simulation, dissimulation, heterosuggestion, more or less avowed self-interest—nothing is lacking to the psychological picture of this subject of possession. We can well understand why Marescot concluded that the subject entrusted to his skill was a case of sheer simulation. But are we now able to take the case further and produce a more accurate diagnosis? We believe it is not presumption to say that we are. Certainly, Marthe must be included in the vast category of the pseudo-demoniacs, but must she be considered a mere impostor? Is her case not partly pathological?

In Marescot's time the pathology of the imagination, which in France has been the subject of such remarkable studies by Ernest Dupré, was still unknown, and hysteria[24] was scarcely mentioned. Nowadays we know far more about the disturbances that can be aroused in an insufficiently controlled imagination, both by emotions and by suggestions, whether from the subject

---

[24]Hysteria is now known as Conversion Disorder.—Ed.

(autosuggestion) or from others (heterosuggestion). More precisely, Dupré has described, under the name "mythomania," that
more or less voluntary and conscious pathological tendency to
falsehood and the creation of imaginary fables. These creations
of the imagination are not confined to the domain of the mind
alone, but can be externalized in the form of simulations of abnormal organic states, which may be considered objective lies,
fables in action. Those who lend themselves to such simulations
deceive with their bodies, and for them should be reserved the
epithet of hysterical or mythoplastic. Marthe Brossier showed
herself to be suffering from both mythomania and hysteria, sensitive to external suggestion and finding in the interest aroused
by her "devilries" a climate pleasing to her vanity.

It need scarcely be said that against disorders of this kind
exorcism must be avoided as useless and even dangerous.

Magdalen of the Cross, of Cordova[25]

To read the checkered career of the woman who for so many
years was the revered prioress of the Poor Clare monastery of
St. Elizabeth at Cordova is like plunging into a novel that is the
product of an unbridled imagination and an incredible simplicity. In fact it is nothing of the sort, and if many of the incidents
now make us smile, the greater number correspond to a real
state of affairs, obviously distorted and exaggerated, but still
founded on symptoms peculiar to deceit and trickery, in fact to
derangement of judgment.

It was in 1487, when the storms of war that had ravaged An-
dalusia were just dying down, that Magdalen saw the light. Her

---

[25]Maurice Garçon, *Madeleine de la Croix, Abbesse diabolique*
(Paris: Sorlot, 1939).

parents were poor and lived at Aguilar, her birthplace. From her earliest infancy, we are told, she was the object of singular phenomena. While she was at prayer in the church, an angel had appeared to her, young, handsome and resplendent with light. At the sight, the little girl stretched out her arms and heard the mysterious visitant give her great encouragements, at the same time signing her on the forehead.

Other manifestations of the same kind soon followed, attracting, as we may guess, the attention of the populace to this little girl, the object of so many heavenly favors. One day, after seeing a vision of Christ in glory, Magdalen ran to the church, knelt down, and fell into an ecstasy, having first cured a poor cripple. People crowded around to look at her in this attitude of mystical rapture. Seeing nothing, indifferent to every external appeal, her arms crossed, Magdalen remained as motionless as a stone.

Still more extraordinary, someone who observed her from close by thought he could see, reflected in her eyes, the image of the Holy Trinity, surrounded by the company of the elect. Coming at last out of this ecstasy, Magdalen declared that she had just been transported into Heaven, where God Himself had told her she had been sanctified from before her birth. Very often, we are told, Magdalen inflicted very severe bodily pains on herself, even to the length of crucifixion. But, marvelous to relate, after the blood had flowed from her hands and feet, the flesh was miraculously closed again. One is not surprised to learn that, like many others of the same temperament, she ceased to take any food for whole months together, her health being none the worse.

Her first Communion was marked by an even greater prodigy: while the rite was in progress, she uttered a loud cry and fell into an ecstatic rapture; her lips closed, her mouth firmly shut, she seemed to be out of this world. While all around her were in a state of agitation, Magdalen opened her mouth, to reveal a host. Such an event, it was believed, could only be the proof of the girl's sanctity, and she was admitted without question to the Poor Clare monastery of St. Elizabeth.

Ecstasies and raptures, which the life of the cloister did nothing to check, naturally marked out the young novice for the attention of the nuns; but what seemed the greatest marvel of all was her Communion which, so Magdalen said, our Lord Himself gave her during the Mass. Whenever the moment of the "miracle" came, she would utter a loud cry, claiming she had seen the Child Jesus Himself in the celebrant's hands. How could anyone doubt the truth of this when the host which she had miraculously received could invariably be seen on her tongue?

Such a profusion of extraordinary favors might have tainted a less fervent soul with pride, but it was remarked precisely that Magdalen continued to be simple in her ways, self-effacing, and of exemplary humility.

Then the monastery was set in a flutter by fresh manifestations: Magdalen was distributing blood-stained bandages which, she said, had been applied to the stigmatic wound in her side. And, of course, all knew that for four years this Poor Clare had taken no nourishment, maintaining this *media* without interruption.

In 1509, at the age of twenty-two, Magdalen was called on to take her perpetual vows. There was a great ceremony, attended by all the most important personages of the district, and it was marked by a marvelous prodigy; a sound of wings was heard, while a dove perched on the floor, seeming to speak to the maiden. The bird remained motionless throughout the ceremony, and when the organs had pealed out and the doors were opened, it flew up into the clear sky, where it circled gracefully until it became an almost invisible speck.

We shall not enlarge on the extraordinary manifestations which ensued in the monastery of St. Elizabeth: all the prodigies we have related were renewed almost monotonously. But in 1518, on the feast of the Annunciation (March 25), Magdalen of the Cross reported that on the previous night she had conceived the Child Jesus by the Holy Spirit. On being informed, the abbess most strictly forbade this news from being repeated, as it would have led to scandal.

Justifiably alarmed, the bishop ordered an inquiry, which established Magdalen's virginity. The months passed by, the professed nun was growing big,[26] but she remained so modest, bearing her burden so unaffectedly that one could not fail to admire her. Christmas came around: on Christmas Eve Magdalen said she was suffering the first pangs of childbirth. The midwives were about to be summoned when the expectant mother declared that her angel ordered her to retire to a little hermitage at the foot of the garden, where she would be delivered alone and in pain. On the morning of the 26th she reappeared and declared that during the night she had given birth to a magnificent babe, from whom flowed a light as bright as daylight. The child had never uttered a cry. The miraculous nature of this

---

[26]Psychiatrists have observed cases today of what is termed, "pseudocyesis," or "false pregnancy," a form of conversion (or hysteria) accompanied by the symptoms of pregnancy, including marked abdominal and breast enlargement, cessation of menses, and other physical symptoms, yet without a true pregnancy. —Ed.

pregnancy and and childbirth seemed all the more certain because, this time too, the midwives had confirmed her virginity.

But in spite of all the proofs which seemed to support the reality of the favors showered on Magdalen of the Cross, some persons were still skeptical. With the authorization of the abbess a monk obtained leave to make an experiment that, no doubt of it, would be decisive. During one of her ecstasies, the monk roughly pierced the nun with two long pins, one in her foot, the other in her hand. She never winced; not a muscle moved. On coming out of her ecstasy, she declared she had felt absolutely nothing.

Proof had been given; these were manifestations surpassing what could be expected from nature alone. God or the devil? These were the two alternatives. Was it the devil? But his influence could be excluded, because an exorcist, delivering a possessed woman from a demon called Sabaoth, had oddly enough received a singular revelation. Questioned on his attitude toward Magdalen of the Cross, Sabaoth had replied with violent insults and maintained that the Poor Clare had been a saint since her conception.

Thus confirmed in her reputation, our heroine enjoyed a prestige in the monastery surpassing that of the abbess. Prodigies, which seemed to be miracles, abounded, yet Magdalen never ceased to be a model of modesty, humility, and devotion.

Urged by her companions to accept the office of abbess, which was about to be vacated, Magdalen, after hesitations that seemed to testify to her modesty, at last accepted. And in 1533 she was called to replace the infirm and incapable abbess and henceforward to rule the monastery. But, once made abbess, she revealed a pitiless and despotic character hitherto unsuspected. Yet, in spite of the fearful penances she imposed, she was reelected in 1535 and 1539. During the whole of this period the prodigies in her regard never ceased; for thirty-five years no priest had ever given her the consecrated host. There was another remarkable fact: having received from St. Francis a special revelation dispensing her from confession, Magdalen had completely abandoned the sacrament of Penance.

But soon, in consequence of some alleged apparitions and revelations of the "Mother of God" which cast doubt on the purity of birth and race of some young novices, public opinion was aroused, and in 1542 she obtained only a paltry number of votes at the election.

In disgrace and placed under strict supervision by the new abbess, Magdalen was convicted of fraud and hoaxing. It was proved, in fact, that she had caused food to be secretly brought to her by a sister in charge of the pantry, who was blindly devoted to her, and that moreover she possessed a secret pyx containing hosts.

Anxious to do nothing without complete certainty, the new abbess, Isabella of the Holy Trinity, made this experiment. While Magdalen was walking in the cloister, some drops of holy water were sprinkled, without her knowledge, on her habit. Seized with sudden convulsions, the former abbess fell to the ground, as if struck by lightning.

The experiment seemed to be decisive, so a confessor was summoned. On seeing him, Magdalen was again seized with convulsions and ended by falling into an ecstasy. A doctor, summoned in haste, was very perplexed, for while deep pricks produced no reaction, piercing with a needle dipped in holy water brought on violent convulsive paroxysms. Rebellious and furious, Magdalen kept on repeating: "Fifteen forty-four, that is the year of the promised forty years.... Cursed, vile dog, will you carry me off to Hell?" Preparing herself for death, Magdalen then made a private confession that so overcame the provincial that his face seemed altered and aged, and horror was depicted on his drawn features.

The affair was so serious that the inquisitor in person was required to receive the confession of the former abbess. Unveiling the blackness of her soul, she made the confession of her whole life, an appalling confession of a lifetime devoted to sin, sacrilege, deceit, fraud, and wickedness.

From the age of five, she declared, she had been vowed to the devil, whose voice "was ever muttering in her ears." This "familiar" devil was called Balban, and was sometimes accompanied by another called Patonio. Sometimes these beings were materialized in the forms of animals: bats, a cock, a pig, a toad, a snake.

After promising obedience to Balban by playing the part of a humble, prudent, and pious nun in the monastery, Magdalen signed a genuine pact with the devil, a pact written on a parchment with her blood. By means of this pact, Magdalen's rise was assured, on condition that she lent herself to all the devil's desires, to all the subterfuges and sacrileges most deeply offensive to the majesty of God. But the devil to whom she had to remain subject had clearly specified that its influence would assure her a period of good fortune only for a space of twenty-five years. This term was about to expire, and the wretched woman would now become a common sinner, without support.

On January 1, 1544, Magdalen was arrested and subjected to exorcisms, which delivered her from Balban. Repentant, she now seemed to grasp the full depth and horror of her sins and made scarcely any difficulty about revealing certain hidden corners of the satanic life she professed to have lived.

The demon? Yes, indeed, it had appeared to her very often: at first in the form of a young man glowing with light, then of a big man, hairy and flaming, finally in the form of a creature with the torso of a man, the face of a faun and the legs of a goat. From its head sprouted two horns which seemed to defy Heaven. To the trembling Magdalen it revealed that the moment had come for her to become its wife, that she could give herself to it without fear, and that her virgin state would never be lost. Taking her in its arms and clasping her fiercely, the devil turned itself again into a handsome young man, and she surrendered herself to it with the utmost license. Ever since then she had been receiving the visits of the incubus-spirit and allowing it to give her unspeakable and shameful pleasures.

But in truth it was not only carnal enjoyments she received from the demon but also ecstasies, which cleverly simulated those of the mystics, but were really of a quite different kind. The devil carried her, divided in herself, to various places far and near. Now it was to the convent of the Franciscans, where she was able to be present at the chapter meetings, then it was on marvelous journeys, to Rome, to Portugal, even to Mexico.

What about the alleged pregnancy? On this point, she was positive: the symptoms she experienced were such that there could be no misunderstanding: daily possessed by the demon, it was not surprising that she should suffer something of this sort, and the demon itself feared some scandal. And so she was relieved when her abdomen was deflated on that Christmas night in 1518.

As for the stigmata with which she pretended she had been marked in the side and hands, she confessed that the wounds had been artificially produced, and that the blood which seemed to flow from them came from another part of her body.

A story of this sort cannot fail to astound the reader unfamiliar with the facts of so-called diabolical possession, but I have described these strange events in some detail only because in our day we can distinguish in this story between the true and the false, the possible and the impossible.

That she consumed hosts without the priest's intervention has already been established, which is not to say that it was anything preternatural. I was once in a position to see a nun who claimed to have the stigmata, and the strange thing was that the wound in her left side contained, on a silken cushion, a host, "like a counter in an automatic distributor," as the superior confided in me. I did not observe it personally, but this was told me by two nuns whose sincerity and competence as observers were unquestionable. What I was able to establish, after the disappearance of this singular phenomenon, was the existence of a thick scar, crescent-shaped, crimping the lower internal side of the left breast. Obviously this scar could only have been produced with a cutting instrument. When questioned, the nun maintained that an angel, or our Lord Himself, had communicated with her in her heart. Magdalen of the Cross frequently fell into trances, from her childhood, and for several minutes would lose all contact with the outer world; after these trances a "sweat of blood" used to soak her wimple and cap. So in this case, too, it was not hard to detect the fraud, for the cloths were not impregnated with blood, but were visibly "daubed."

In the course of her ecstasies this person was, she claimed, the recipient of very particular visions: a personage, always of the same appearance, young and handsome, appeared to her and spoke words to her, sometimes asking her to read some passage of the Gospels, sometimes reminding her that while it was good to pray to Jesus Christ, one must not forget God the

Father. The first personage differed from the second by carrying a cross or making the Sign of the Cross, while the second was not distinguished by any mark. As for the third character, his proposals were revoltingly obscene, and this was the devil.

The connection between this nun and Magdalen of the Cross is that both were thought to be models of sanctity and both became superiors of their order, promoted over the heads of their contemporaries.

In her general confession Magdalen of the Cross (whom Maurice Garçon does not hesitate to call "the diabolical abbess") proclaimed that the demon separated her soul from her fleshly body and transported it to very distant places, so that it was present at scenes to which mortal man had not access.

Now in chapter 10 of his book will be found the very strange but perfectly true story of a pious woman who, possessed by a demon during the nights, was convinced that her being could be separated into two parts, one comprising her fleshly body, the other its double. The demon possessed the latter in the same manner in which it possessed Magdalen, giving her unspeakable delights which covered her with horror, shame, and confusion, for she was still deeply attached to her Christian faith. Furthermore, the devil transported her into what she called "the Astral." There, this poor creature was made the victim of the most abominable outrages and the cruelest atrocities, which affected her fleshly body. There Sibylle (for so she was called) witnessed scenes we cannot describe, which plumbed the very depths of horror.

It seems to me, therefore, that the incredible story of Magdalen of the Cross is based on true facts, wrongly interpreted. Obviously, the real is here mixed with the magical, the imaginary, the fictional; but if the most extravagant elements composing the life of the diabolical abbess are true, they were actualized by a perverse imagination in a hysterical and mythomanic personality.

The Convulsionaries

As we have indicated earlier, what has given rise to belief in the invasion of a person's body by an evil spirit, by the demon or the devil, has always been the unexpected appearance of extraordinary manifestations, so different from the person's apparent nature that it would seem really difficult not to seek and find a preternatural or supernatural origin for them. And since this type of possession could not be from God, because of its consequences, it was deemed inevitable to ascribe it to the influence of the "evil spirit."

Those convulsive attacks, so terrifying in all their accompanying circumstances, certainly correspond with what we have described under the title of the "paroxysmal form of demonopathic pseudo-possession," of epileptic or hysterical type, but the events we are now to discuss are not isolated, sporadic paroxysms, but regular epidemics. The convulsionary is no longer a personal entity, he is Legion. The question which therefore arises is: Can the origin and spreading of the demonopathic attacks be considered as merely individual events, or do they justify belief in the reality of a genuine influence of the demon?

It is remarkable that epidemics of demoniacal attacks always appear in a religious context, in the most general sense of the term. This explains the dilemma that has so wrongly misled inquiry into the origin and nature of convulsive paroxysms. "God or the devil?" men asked, without inquiring, as would have been reasonable, whether simulation, mental contagion, and, above all, suggestion, were not the sources of the violent manifestations that, by their excesses and scandals, so alarmed the religious authorities and were a natural object of concern to the representatives of the civil power.

The scale of this work does not allow me to quote the numerous "epidemics of demonopathy" of a cataclysmic nature that have occurred both in France and elsewhere. Such would indeed be tediously repetitive, for the initial process is always the same: the contagion takes effect according to general laws, the strictness of which is now generally known. I shall venture only to give a brief sketch of some demonopathic epidemics, so as to point out the dangers that may arise from a mistaken interpretation of the events and from a lack of strictness in the observation of the facts and the preventive measures.

The Convulsionaries of the Cemetery of Saint-Medard

There can scarcely be any more striking example of mental contagion than the story of the extraordinary manifestations, so grotesque, scandalous, and terrifying, which took place at the beginning of the eighteenth century, the "Age of Enlightenment."

These events occurred at the tomb of the deacon François de Paris, who had rendered up his soul to God while still young: he was only thirty-seven at his death on May 2, 1727.[27] A pronounced Jansenist, he had never ceased to subject himself to

---

[27] The work that gives the most striking observations on the manifestations at the tomb of the deacon Paris is still that by Carré de Montgeron, in two volumes, one published in 1737, the second in 1741, entitled *De la vérité des miracles opérés à l'intercession de M. de Pâris et autres appelans, démontrée contre l'Archevêque de Sens*. The text is embellished with remarkable engravings.

mortifications, fasts, and the severest bodily penances, until they brought about his death. He was therefore very soon considered to be a model of sanctity.

On May 3, 1727, his mortal remains were laid in one of the cemeteries which at that time flanked the church of Saint-Medard. In no time there were devout believers, pilgrims, and sick people flocking there to pray and to seek for the cure of diseases that had baffled doctors. Very soon, too, extraordinary phenomena began to appear at the holy deacon's tomb. These, being regarded as evidence of some more or less preternatural power, were made the subject of numerous police reports which, being recorded in a simple, direct style, may be taken as the quite objective description of what happened at Saint-Medard.[28] The police informers (the "mouches") were soon protesting in the name of morality: "The most scandalous thing about it is to see girls, pretty and well developed, whose immodest attitudes are such as to excite certain passions." It hardly needs repeating that it was just the same with the convulsionaries of Loudun.

Public opinion, too, was aroused, and the scenes occurring at the deacon's tomb were subjected to an ever stricter police supervision. We thus possess, in these police reports, very valuable documents on the diversity and nature of these manifestations, for which the veneration of the deacon Paris was the pretext. Soon, so-called miraculous cures of ulcers, cancer, and palsy reinforced belief in the reality of a mysterious source of supernatural power, objectified, so to speak, in the immortal and still-present soul of the "Blessed de Paris."

[28]I take these documents from the book by Albert Mousset: *L'Étrange histoire des convulsionnaires de Saint-Medard* (Paris: Éditions de Minuit, 1953).

Paroxysmal Forms of Pseudo-Diabolical Possession

As he himself had been subject to nervous attacks that his neighbors described as "convulsions," paroxysmal attacks of the same kind took place at his tomb. A very mixed multitude was attracted to the cemetery by motor disorders, very varied and extravagant, and very puzzling in the mystery of their nature. Believers and fanatics could be seen, as well as the curious and the skeptical, and undesirable characters, and finally the police and the clergy. We are not surprised to learn that women were much more numerous than men, although the latter were not spared.

What were the outward phenomena expressing the changes of personality that seemed so astounding and so disconcerting? A muscular agitation of the whole body, so acute that it was incomprehensible how such a paroxysm could be violently produced in a person who seemed to be neither ill nor possessed by the devil. We read in a police report: "Some lively movements, turning of the head, gestures with the hands, as if writing or drawing. Carries the right hand to the mouth, opens it and puts the two first fingers in it … then raises both hands and crosses them on the breast; lies quietly stretched out on the couch; is then seized with hiccoughs and strikes out with both hands in all directions and imitates fighting; is terrified and complains, saying: 'O God, that is terrible!'"[29]

It is significant that the convulsive episode was often preceded by a period of meditation, a sort of calm before the storm that was about to burst. Then the trance came on rapidly. In the midst of extraordinary convulsions the patient uttered cries, muttered incoherent words, fell on her knees, besought God, while those present redoubled their prayers.

[29]Ibid., 122.

True or False Possession?

With many of those concerned, what we might call the "muscular storm" was such that a master surgeon, Louis Sivert, declared "that he had seen certain convulsionaries at Saint-Medard making such strange movements that a man could not possibly make them voluntarily. For example, spinning their heads as if on a pivot and with great speed, and sometimes to be found with their noses between their shoulders."

Could not the source of such manifestations be found in the work of the devil? This was the question asked all the more insistently as it seemed clear that mere human powers were being exceeded. For example, there was a frequenter of the cemetery, Abbé Becheran de la Motte, a venerable priest afflicted with complete atrophy of the left leg; he attended the cemetery so assiduously that the spectators wondered if they witnessed a saint or a possessed man. The sergeants of the guard responsible for supervising him reported:

> Abbé Becheran came to the tomb about eleven in the morning, accompanied by several clerics and his lackeys; they laid him on the tomb with two cushions under him, then they chanted psalms and the Abbé was seized with about twenty-two convulsions. He made sudden starts and *diabolic demonstrations*, enough to make one tremble; he bit himself and gnashed his teeth and behaved as only a madman could. (Another day the unfortunate visitor to the tomb remained about an hour and a half:) there were five men to make him jump. He struggled and made fearful shrieks, saying the alphabet backwards: *hu, ho, hi, he, ha,* and making grimaces like a madman.

As we remarked, there were all sorts among the crowds at Saint-Medard, female healers, coprophagists who thought they were mortifying themselves, makers of plaster statues, "sec-ouristes" of the first or second rank, for the poor folk in their trances must of course be helped and protected from wounding themselves. But, as was to happen later around the famous tub, where the charlatan Mesmer dispensed his fluid of animal magnetism, it was not long before erotic displays began, which were bound to give credence to the idea of diabolical influence. Clad in floating garments so as not to impede their demonstrations, these girls, with complete shamelessness,

> performed their leaps, capers and somersaults, and forced the spectators to see what should never be seen. Men put their feet on their arms, their thighs, their necks and even their eyes; they carry them by the feet with cords, and their disheveled heads shake, spin and hang for some time as if motionless. Again men rush at them like fighting rams and butt them in the breast with their heads; they invite blows with the fist or a log,... one uncovers her shoulders to show the shudderings in her spine, another her back to point out the same lines as are seen in her face.

Such were the effects of what was called the "grand secours." But many of the convulsionaries dissociated themselves from such scenes or opposed them. That was the line of one of the most formidable "anti-secouristes," Françoise Lefebvre d'Ecouen. She had a great reputation, and she not only thought the "grand secours" to be the work of the devil but claimed that one day she had distinctly seen Satan crouching on the body of his victim.

Such circumstances naturally seemed attributable, more and more urgently, to the maleficent influence of the demon. Are we so sure, wrote an anonymous author, of the fate of M. de Paris? If it is really a saint who is behind the prodigies taking place at Saint-Medard, why does it please a merciful God to cause so many unfortunates to suffer, "innocents in good faith, who come to pray through the intercession of a man they believe to be a saint"?

"The very manner in which the cripples try to be cured would seem more striking than the miracles, since in the strength of their obsessions they themselves stretch out their poor shortened or bent limbs, in the attempt to lengthen or straighten them."

So a great mystery hung over the faith and the destiny of these convulsionaries, and the riddle inevitably propounded by the solid fact of the convulsions seemed all the more difficult to solve because the unfortunate victims swore that they remembered nothing of what happened during their seizures.

God or Satan? That was the dilemma confronting the theorists, both lay and clerical. Nonetheless, there were some who refused to believe in the supernatural origin of the convulsions and put them down to trickery or even to the major neurosis, hysteria.

Thus an anonymous author[30] declared himself convinced, after the year 1731, that the singular manifestations at Saint-Medard did not depend on any intervention, divine or demoniacal, but were the effect of purely natural causes. "What has always struck me," writes this author, "was to see that the majority of the convulsionaries were of that sex which we know to

[30]*Observations sur l'origine et le progrès des convulsions qui ont commencé au cimetière de Saint-Medard. Oit l'on montre qu'elles sont des effets naturels, et que rien n'oblige a les regarder comme divines* (April 21, 1733).

be very susceptible to the impressions of objects, and to have a very mobile imagination, which the slightest things can often excite very powerfully." On the other hand, a certain M. Maupoint, a convulsionary who had been imprisoned in the Bastille, was asked to demonstrate the extraordinary movements of his head that he had made during his attacks. This patient, "having very willingly agitated and shaken his head so as to represent them somehow, had at once fallen into convulsions, in which he had the most rapid and surprising turnings of the head. It is obvious that he did not have them voluntarily, but that the whole nervous system was tense in him and ready to enter into convulsion, and this slight movement of the head had been the occasion of a general release, which had caused these alarming convulsions."

Recalling the observations of Thomas Willis concerning hysterical subjects, our author remarks that, in contrast with convulsive paroxysms (for example, epilepsy), the patients on coming out of their trance feel no discomfort or exhaustion. When the crisis is over, "the patient is as well as before, they [the attacks] do not affect the health."

One cannot but admire the high qualities as observer and critic of this author, who wished to remain anonymous. Long before Charcot and his school, he saw clearly that many alleged demoniacs were only hysterical subjects, inclined to suffer the effects of suggestion, that the convulsive paroxysms could be *induced* or provoked by an attempt at voluntary repetition of the attack, and finally that the trances had no bad effect on the general health.

Nowadays we would draw the conclusion that the manifestations at Saint-Medard, which many enlightened persons thought to be prodigies, were not all produced by the same mechanism. Some no doubt sprang from *hysteria major*, the "demoniacal attack" of Charcot and Paul Richer; others seem to me to be produced by more or less conscious simulation, by mythomania associated with mythoplastia, while the rest show the effects of mental contagion among the weak-minded. But the influence of the demon is to be sought in vain.

The Convulsionaries of the Ursuline Convent at Loudun

With these scenes, at once picturesque, absurd, loathsome and pitiful, which developed at the cemetery of Saint-Medard at the tomb of the deacon Paris, we may associate the events, now quite devoid of mystery, which excited so many controversies and violent quarrels at the beginning of the seventeenth century: I mean the phenomena of supposed collective possession among the Ursulines of Loudun. In this case as in the other, a very mixed public, which included fanatics, skeptics, mystifiers, and the merely curious, looked on at very strange scenes, blended of tragedy and comedy, which to us seem profoundly afflicting.

The sad story, outlined above, of Jeanne de Berciel, prioress of the Ursuline monastery at Loudun, shows what serious dangers are incurred by allowing persons suffering from convulsions, whatever their nature, to live together. Either the epileptics, by their alarming convulsive paroxysms, induce in emotional and hysterical subjects the reproduction—imperfect but similar and deceptive—of the epileptic attacks (as happened at the Salpêtrière Hospital before the arrival of Charcot), or else the demonopath, who is subject to lurid psychomotor manifestations, impresses his mark on a whole community. This is precisely what we learn from the story of the supposedly possessed women at Loudun. In those days exorcism was not only in common use but was carried out in public, a course which we now know could only exacerbate the agitation and theatricality of the possessed.

Observe that the disordered movements, stamped with delirium of the senses, were an exact reproduction of those known to Greek antiquity in the Sibyl's cave or the temple of the Pythian oracle. They were the same convulsions so perfectly described by Charcot and Richer and personally observed by me in a great many patients during the First World War.

Their essential traits are as follows. Imagine that after a period marked by rigidity extending to the whole body, and gnashings of the teeth so violent as to break them, there follows a phase of wild, clownish movements, during which the convulsive patient expresses rage and fury, shouts, struggles, insults, blasphemes, curses, seems literally mad—and we still have only a faint image of what Charcot and Richer called the major demoniacal-hysterical crisis. One would really think that the person was suddenly transformed, that an alien influence was controlling him and providing him with strength, skill, daring, and inventions, which his own nature could not provide.

This severe attack is sometimes followed by a very particular phenomenon, which observers of the demonopathic attacks have admirably clarified—namely, ecstasy. All the muscular storm and the extravagant, picturesque, or terrifying clownishness are now stilled; with eyes open, the gaze fixed on emptiness, the subject seems plunged in a dream, ceases to answer questions, does not react when pinched or pricked. He is really rapt away from the real world, lost in a sort of sleep, which is nourished by sensorial, visual, and auditory hallucinations. But in a somewhat confused manner it is possible to guess the meaning of the interior drama of which the patient is both the theater and the actor. Then follows the reawakening, the resumption of contact with reality, without the recent storm leaving the slightest ill effect on the subject's personality—contrary to the effect of epilepsy.

I have recapitulated the essential notes of the major demoniacal attack in hysterical patients, because this is precisely what we find fully active in those convulsionaries, the "possessed" of Loudun and elsewhere.

Now, as I have already emphasized, the major demoniacal attack, more than any other manifestation, seems liable to diffusion and imitation, especially at certain times and in certain surroundings. The sixteenth and seventeenth centuries appear to have been especially favorable to them, but exactly the same manifestations occurred at the tomb of the deacon Paris, at the Salpêtrière in the time of Charcot, and later in the neuropsychiatric centers of France, during the 1914-1918 war.

As early as 1630, most of the observers scarcely believed in levitation any longer, but they were still impressed by the grotesque contortions, the wild gesticulations, and the acrobatic exploits displayed by the unfortunate religious, and not least by their mother prioress. I need not repeat the description quoted earlier by M. de Nion.

Critical and Clinical Study of the State of
Consciousness during Paroxysmal Possession

There is no need to exaggerate, but the great advances made in our knowledge about the eternal problem of self-knowledge, of our consciousness, our ego, our underlying personality are undeniable. But if we imagine ourselves back in the epoch in which the demonopathic incidents occurred, we shall be less astonished at the singular errors of judgment made by the observers. Man's nature was conceived as made of a body and a soul, the soul being indivisible and immortal, and so, when a human being appeared to be transformed in his personality, it could only be by some process beyond the reach of human nature. The appearance of several alternating personalities in the same person could not yet be imagined. And when the behavior of a person who did not seem to be a real lunatic struck everyone by its singularity and wild vagaries, men were led to look for its cause either in divine action or in some diabolical power, since all our acts derived "from God, or from the devil, or from ourselves."

Take, for example, a woman who falls suddenly into lethargy or catalepsy, her limbs preserving the rigidity of marble or bronze; one may prick her or pinch her, and she remains unconscious until a breath on her eyes recalls her to life.

Or take a girl who, in contrast with her usual behavior, her position as a nun, her constant piety, utters insulting, obscene, and blasphemous words, who gesticulates, falls to the ground, and shakes herself with the utmost immodesty; yet when the attack has passed she recovers an apparently normal equilibrium. Is it credible, people would then say, that this transformation of the personality, of this "ego" whose permanence is the essential condition of the continuity of the psychological life, does not prove the intrusion of another occult "entity," which can only be diabolical?

Certain skeptics, I know, asked whether some fraud did not take place, which could have explained the supposedly demoniacal manifestations; but all the observation (imperfect as it was in those days, giving us nothing precise) seemed to attest the absolute sincerity of the subjects.[31] We may add that often the observers only remembered as much of the subject's behavior as they wished to find there.

On the other hand, they had not progressed beyond the doctrine of Descartes, according to which the soul, although it acts on the body, cannot directly affect the body of another; so that even such phenomena as telepathy and telekinesis, which certain modern scientists and philosophers admit to be possible or probable, were not envisaged. It was therefore absolutely necessary to fall back, in the last analysis, on the influence of a supernatural entity: God or the devil, and especially Satan.

We of today have come a long way from the Cartesian psychophysiology, which denied souls to the beasts and mocked so wittily at Jean de la Fontaine. What Descartes refused to see in man was the fragility of his personality, his passive division, his successive transformations, in certain persons; in short, the whole field of that psychological activity which is subconscious, subliminal or unconscious.

Let us return to the state, or rather states, of consciousness of those subjects we are obliged to consider neuropathic or hysterical demoniacs.

One first point is undeniable: certain demonopathic crises or attacks are purely theatrical: the subject is simply a more or less clever actress and often a mythomaniac in action, who remains lucidly aware of her vagaries. Marie-Thérèse Noblet,

---

[31] Together with Fr. Bruno de Jésus-Marie, I have shown how supervision over a possessed person can be cleverly evaded by a hysterical patient, and all neurologists know that one must attribute to this neurosis only what one observes directly, at first hand, and not all of that! These hysterical subjects are able to deceive the best observers.

after a great convulsive attack, sufficiently dramatic to make Fr. Eschimann think she was in her agony, asked him ironically: "Father, weren't you afraid?"—like a mother amusing her child.

At other times, the state of consciousness is quite different: the patient leaves the world of reality in order to plunge into a world that can best be compared to that of dreams or hypnosis. The possessed person acts, it is said, like an automaton. Yes, but with this difference: that while consciousness of the self is suspended, consciousness of the external world, such as an animal possesses, persists. The demonopathic state, in short, appears quite like that of the somnambulist or the hypnotized person. This explains the fact that while the epileptic, in the course of a psychomotor attack, is capable of wounding himself seriously and even killing himself, the hysteric does himself only superficial damage,[32] even though the blows he gives himself when "the devil has hold of him" appear very violent.

But if (as I remarked earlier) the crises are intensified, or if the major demonopathic attack (so perfectly described by Charcot and Richer) comes on, consciousness of the self is weakened and extinguished, rather after the manner of epilepsy, although the two kinds of crisis should never be confused.

Two patients, famous for their convulsive and theatrical attacks, who were studied by Charcot and Richer, were themselves able to distinguish certain "attacks they called their wrigglings from others which were the major attacks." They could even foretell, from the intensity of the phenomena of the

[32]Modern psychiatry recognizes this as one of the key distinctions between true epileptic seizures and (conversion) pseudo-seizures. Those who suffer the former will often, for example, bite their tongue or injure themselves falling, while those who suffer the latter somehow evade serious injury.—Ed.

aura, the kind of attack they were going to have. They much preferred the major attacks to the wrigglings; in the former they completely lost consciousness, while in the latter they lost it only for some moments at a time (during the epileptoid period) and complained that they suffered the most fearful torments imaginable.

After reading the following description by Paul Richer,[33] it is impossible to doubt that *hysteria major* exactly reproduces all the disorders we have described among the most typical cases of possession.

> All of a sudden, appalling cries and shrieks are heard; the body, alive with motions of contortion or stiff in tetanic immobility, carries out strange movements: the legs cross and uncross, the arms are turned back and seem twisted, the fists are clenched, some of the fingers are clenched, some extended, the body bends and rebends in an arc of a circle, or folds and squirms; the head is thrown back to right or left, or held far back, displaying a swollen neck. The face expresses fear, anger, madness, by turns; it is swollen, purple; the eyes open wide, remain fixed or roll in their orbits, often showing only the white of the sclera; the lips are parted, are drawn in opposite directions, revealing a swollen, protruding tongue.... When anger seizes her, she hurls herself at the obstacle, trying to overcome it, strangle it, bite it; often she turns on herself, she pulls out her hair, scratches her face or her breast, tears her clothes and, during this distressful scene, accentuates and accompanies it with cries of sorrow and rage. The patient has completely lost consciousness.

[33]*Études cliniques sur la grande hystérie* (1885).

After Charcot's death, during that period which too often follows the death of great men and might be called the period of ingratitude for their memory, many neurologists (under the influence of Babinski, one of the most eminent disciples of the Master of the Salpêtrière), came to doubt the sincerity of these major theatrical manifestations and wondered whether the whole scene were not produced at will. On this point the skeptics must have been undeceived by what they observed in the great neurological centers during the 1914-1918 war. In fact, the major hysteria, as described by Charcot and his pupils, was seen to revive.

In company with my lamented friend Dr. Henri Claude, I myself observed many examples of the major hysterical attack. Then, as formerly, one witnessed a living drama, and the spectator could not help being frightened at the violence of the blows the poor patient inflicted on himself, heedless of partly healed wounds and risking breaking a callus in course of cicatrization. On a final analysis, on the basis of the cases I directly observed during that war, with Henri Claude, I support the opinion that, although certain hysterical attacks may not considerably, or at all, affect consciousness, there are others that disturb it deeply. After the attack, so the patient declares (and we may believe him), he has forgotten everything which occurred in him and around him during the crisis.

This is the conclusion reached also by T.K. Oesterreich although my thesis differs notably in some points from his. According to Oesterreich,[34] "the possessed do not always, or even generally, preserve a clear consciousness of their fits. It

[34]T.K. Oesterreich, *Possession, Demoniacal and Other* (London: Kegan Paul, 1950).

is the 'demon' alone which expresses itself by their mouths during the fits, and the normal individuality has totally disappeared." In support of this thesis, Oesterreich quotes the cases of demonopathy very well reported on by Eschenmeyer who, on the ground of eight personal observations, professes that the loss of consciousness must be regarded as the essential characteristic of a certain type of possession. "The sudden loss of consciousness, and a total ignorance of what has taken place during the fit," such are the criteria of the type of "possession" I have in mind.

It should be added that the cases on which Oesterreich bases his thesis are the more instructive in that they are those of childhood, that age which is so sensitive to suggestion, hypnosis, somnambulism, and neuropathic accidents.

But we must be careful to note that if the dissolution of consciousness during hysterical paroxysms were as complete as in epilepsy, the patient would scarcely experience any of the feelings of possession, even if he had externalized its most apparent manifestations. It follows, then, that some traces of the change of personality remain in the consciousness and memory, and this, in fact, is proved by analysis of the facts I have personally observed.

A little girl of ten was going on pilgrimage to a celebrated chapel in her district when she thought she saw in front of her the figures of our Lady, the Child Jesus, and St. Joseph. The image was so clear that the child was afraid to go forward on the path for fear of hurting the Child, who was playing in front of His parents.

Later on, she saw demons, the damned, the flames of Hell; she described them very well and in perfect sincerity, sharing these visions first with her brother, then with her mother. We note that this child, devout and well balanced, was so surprised to find herself favored with such visions that she asked, at first, if she had not been dreaming. In fact, the sight she saw was like the most appalling nightmare: she says that after seeing Jesus hanging on His Cross, near His mother, she saw the ground open, and a great billow of smoke appeared, mixed with flames. There she saw people in heaps, weeping and groaning, all mixed up together, and if any of them tried to rise, the devil, seated on a throne, armed with a long fork, pushed them back into the fire. The devil was all red, with red eyes, a red tongue, etc. ... pointed wings, and horns.

The child was very frightened and disturbed for days after this vision of devils and hell. But it must be added that although this child, whose visions went on for a long time, preserved the clearest possible recollection of the scenes which had impressed her, sometimes the cataleptic attitude disappeared suddenly: the child fell to the ground, seeming to sleep, for so long that one day she was found on the ground by some workmen who were passing that way; she would remain in ecstasy, her mother said, for hours, unable to say how long this state had continued. In spite of the great frequency of the apparitions, this child was not deeply disturbed in her conduct, but the influence of these visions on others was not long in taking effect and even became alarming.

Here is another example, this time of a nun whose life in some respects resembles that of Sr. Jeanne of the Angels. Like her, this sister was nominated prioress of her order considerably in advance of the legal age, which means that her conduct was considered specially edifying. Now this religious, on falling into ecstasy, used to have visions of God the Father and God the Son, but alternating with this she sometimes perceived a third personage, with the same appearance as the other two, but this one uttered only obscene words. It was well known that since adolescence this nun used to fall several times a day into "ecstatic" states, during which her spirit seemed to be rapt from the earth and lost in a world unknown to ordinary mortals. The demonopathic phenomena were complicated by many other symptoms that leave no doubt as to the really neuropathic nature of this strange behavior.

Another nun whom I had occasion to observe attracted my attention because of the troubles she experienced during sleep. These consisted in a feeling of "trance," of escape from ordinary sleep. This patient told me: "Then Jesus draws me to one side and I draw myself to the other, so as not to yield to the ecstasy. When this ecstasy develops, I seem to be the prey of the demon, but Jesus has promised to enclose me in a box where Satan will never be able to reach me. Yes, the devil will make me commit many outward faults, but I shall not sin, because my will has nothing to do with them."

In this case, too, the subject wondered whether she had not been dreaming. In any case, we can say that during these trances the state of consciousness is very far from normal, for while the memory of certain crises remains pretty clear, there are others of which the recollection is blurred or extinguished.

I related in the *Études Carmélitaines*[35] the very instructive observation of a girl whose writings and outward piety seemed to indicate that she was in the way of sanctity. When the religious authorities began to pay closer attention to her, stigmata appeared on her forehead, from which bleedings took place

---

[35]Jean Lhermitte, "Les pseudo-possessions démoniaques," in *Satan*; English trans., 280-299.

every Friday. But just when this girl seemed to be nearer to the mystical life, diabolical attacks began. Thus, suddenly one night it seemed as if a man leaped in front of her bed, while the electric light went out and the room was lit with a reddish glow. The strange thing was, she said, "that the eyes of this person followed me, and his body shifted about according as I myself moved." As we may guess, she hastened to tell all these strange facts to her director, "who did not understand."

My eminent friend Fr. Bruno, who on several successive Fridays had been able to observe the bleeding from the forehead, begged the girl to come on Friday to my surgery, after being supervised very closely by an intelligent girl of perfect good faith. This supervisor, who followed Madeleine (the patient) everywhere and even shared her room, told us that openings had formed on her forehead, whence bleeding flowed, on several Fridays in succession. But what struck this observer still more was the multiplicity of the demon's assaults. If they went into a church, she said, the chairs moved, the curtains of the confessional shook violently.

"I have seen Madeleine's shoes removed without her moving; a chair charred while Madeleine, who was sitting on it, was not burned. One night, an extraordinary thing happened: I was awakened out of a quiet sleep by a cry; Madeleine turned on the electric light, took out a packet and put out the light. Immediately there was a smell of burning, and Madeleine showed me a half-burnt chemise."

Convinced, contrary to our supervisor's statements, that all these phenomena were only fabrications, we asked Madeleine to come one Friday to my surgery, where she would be received by Fr. Bruno and me. Our hope was disappointed, for the same morning we received a letter, from which I quote this passage:

For more than six months I have been in interior conflict with the demon; it was a ruthless struggle between the spirit of God, who urged me to good, and another spirit, which flung me into evil. All these stories you have heard are just a continual lie, and I only wish I could tell you what misery I am in.... I have let myself be persuaded more and more often, obliged to speak, to act against myself. I have imagined all these stories, for what motive I do not know, and I feel more and more unhappy, being unable to speak as I should wish to. I have never had terrible visions of the devil, but at certain times I felt him close to me. It was he who made me burn my chemise in spite of myself. *I do not remember.*

This confession should be compared with that of Sr. Jeanne of the Angels, who appeared one day, during the trial of Urbain Grandier, clad only in a shift, in pouring rain, to make honorable amends, and who wrote: "If obedience were to allow me, I should describe with great pleasure all my maladies in detail: hypocrisy, duplicity, arrogance, self-esteem, and self-seeking with all my other vices, in order to oblige those who might read this writing to plead for mercy from the divine justice, which I have so many times offended."

The confession of Sr. Magdalen of the Cross, and the revelations published during her trial, are of the same kind.

Such observations demonstrate how difficult it is to obtain such complete supervision as one would desire, and how skeptical one should remain before admitting the genuineness of diabolical attacks or apparitions.

Here is another example which will show the extreme difficulty of observing certain phenomena too readily ascribed to the activity of the devil. Long before this last incident, there was a nun who, in the middle of the night, in the silence of the monastery, used to cause a great disturbance. Her cell suddenly resounded with strange noises and was sometimes filled with uproar. The bed table was violently overturned and crashed heavily on the carpet; a windowpane was shattered. When this had happened several times, alarm was felt and the nuns tried to reconstruct the order of events; the complete disorder, the noise of the pane breaking, finally the fall of the nun, who was always found wrapped in her coverlet and hidden under her bed. She was supervised more and more strictly without any explanation being found of what happened in the silence of the night.

The mother superior, the superior general, and the sisters of the monastery all refused to believe that the evil one had any share in these stormy scenes. But how, it was asked, could any-one so completely wreck the furniture of her room and break a windowpane before being found wrapped in her coverlet under her bed? A nun was put to watch her in the same room up to four o'clock in the morning; nothing happened, but half an hour later the uproar broke out as before.

The superior general, wishing to clear up this mystery, spent the night in a room adjoining that of the self-styled victim of possession. In the middle of the night, suddenly, the noise broke out, the superior rushed in, but it was too late, the scene was finished. And it is rather remarkable that there was nothing about this sister to show the slightest psychological unbalance. Modest, devout, sound in judgment, apparently open, this sister gave absolutely no sign which might have suggested possession or mythomania. Placed in a clinic, she preserved her serenity and always refused to give any explanation of the events that had disturbed the quiet of her monastery, other than the intervention of the demon. But after this nothing abnormal ever disturbed the course of her nights.

The case of Sibylle[36]

As the reader may have observed in the course of this work, demonopathic manifestations show a singular preference for the hours of night, when sleep invades the destined victim, detaching him from the outside world. For this reason the patient very often wonders whether he has been dreaming. It was therefore with the greatest interest that I followed the development of the supposedly diabolical manifestations in a woman (briefly mentioned earlier) who was referred to me by Fr. de Tonquédec, a learned exorcist and an expert in matters of psychiatry.

This patient's case, which I have described at length in my work devoted to the image of the body, is characterized by the following traits. About the age of thirty, the most curious symptoms appeared. Almost every night, Sibylle was carried by a sort of ecstasy or trance into a world that had nothing in common with the real one; it was, according to her expression, the world of "the Astral." In reality, the woman told us, she felt herself divided into two parts during these trances: one, the earthly body, which stayed in her bed; the other, which was carried off into the Astral.

But, although separated, these two halves of her personality were not unconnected, for the mischiefs to which the astral body was exposed were reflected in the real body. Justifiably alarmed at this "doubling," as she called it, she went to consult

[36]For further details, see my *L'image de notre corps* (Nouvelle Revue critique, 1939).

an occultist, who would give no explanation. Then as a faithful Christian she approached Fr. de Tonquédec, who asked me to advise her.

Sibylle, an intelligent and lucid young woman, who lived with her parents and helped with the housekeeping, told me on many occasions about the nocturnal phenomena she experienced. At my request she wrote two exercise books, in which the following incidents are described.

After going to bed, determined to fall asleep, Sibylle was carried away into what she called the Astral. She took the name from a book picked up by chance from a bookstall on the quays. There, in the Astral, her "double" suffered continuously the assaults and outrages of the demon. Whether the evil spirit appeared in its natural form, or disguised, or transformed into foul beasts and especially snakes, it subjected her to the most humiliating, cynical, pestering, and even painful attacks. The devil forced her to enter a "diabolic club," where they abused her, giving her erotic sensations which she struggled by every means to avoid, but her will remained helpless. They burned her astral body (the double) and at once her earthly body felt the pain and the scorching; they abandoned themselves to truly satanic "experiments" on her. Thus the demon appeared under the form of a bearded creature which beat her or sent her snakes, which entered her body. But it was the erotic assaults which mortified the poor girl unspeakably. The demon took her in its arms, violated her like a mortal man, and gave her sensations the more terrifying as they seemed the more delicious. Sometimes the devil disguised itself as a priest, who made her suffer the same amorous tortures. Again, the demon tied her up to make her suffer, still in her astral double, burned her hair, threw her into a thorn bush, shot at her.

True or False Possession?

Needless to say, in order to defend herself from these diabolical devices, Sibylle invoked the "protecting powers": God, our Lady, the saints, and used countless means to chase the demon from her room: a brazier was placed under her bed, or a piece of burnt sugar; two rosaries were round her arms; from time to time she drank holy water so that her double might be restored to her. This idea of the dispossession of her own double was so strong and so real that one night, wishing to get up to leave her bed, she could stand up only with the greatest trouble and tottered helplessly, her double having been taken from her.

It is not surprising to learn that, in spite of all these bodily cruelties inflicted on her by the evil spirit, it was always impossible to discover the slightest trace of tegumentary lesions. One day, however, Sibylle sought me out to show me the authentic mark of the demon, the *Sigillum diaboli*. "Last night," Sibylle told me, "the demon launched a specially furious attack on me; it scratched my chest with its nails and claws, so that when my double came back, its application to my earthly body caused me frightful pain." Examining Sibylle's chest I was able to observe a very recent vesicular eruption of shingles in the region of the fifth and sixth left dorsal roots.

There can be little doubt that in certain surroundings and at certain periods this mark would have been thought significant. But Sibylle's story appears even more interesting from another point of view: that of the origin of this psychopathy. At the age of ten, Sibylle suffered from epidemic encephalitis. Treated in a Paris hospital, she was discharged apparently cured, although she retained some slight character troubles. Still more remarkable, after these nocturnal troubles which lasted for some years, her state deteriorated and she had to be placed in a psychiatric hospital, where she rejoined her mother, who had suffered for years from *dementia praecox*,[37] a disease to which she herself succumbed.

I have compared the case of Sibylle with the earlier ones, which are very different in nature, simply in order to make it clear that certain organic states are capable of producing very curious disturbances of the personality, through the deceptions of dreams. Sibylle was of course dreaming when her double was carried into the Astral, but the dream here took on very individual characteristics. In spite of attempts from outside, Sibylle did not recover contact with reality. I asked her father to observe her during these trance states, which was very easy. And he told me that his daughter, plunged in a sort of ecstasy, seemed positively rapt out of the real world; her eyes, though open, saw nothing outside her, while her gaze seemed to be directed by some inward representation, exactly as happens in sleepwalking.

No doubt it would be extremely difficult, and in fact impossible, to realize for oneself the remarkably strange state into which Sibylle plunged during her nights. As Charles Blondel has shown, a normal consciousness can never become capable of flowing into the mold of a morbid consciousness, short of becoming such itself. But the fact of it remains.

It is obvious that nothing would be more unreal than to try to include in one formula the states of consciousness of these possessed persons. We may agree, however, that while the major paroxysms develop in a consciousness wholly detached from the links binding it to the external world, and even the memory

---

[37]*Dementia praecox*, a term popularized by the great nineteenth-century psychiatrist Emil Kraepelin, is now known as schizophrenia. It is characterized by chronic psychosis, or loss of contact with reality (for example, in the form of hallucinations, delusions, or grossly disorganized thinking). —Ed.

of the picture of the crisis may vanish during the commonest "attacks," the patient does not fail to reveal himself as both spectator and actor in the same drama.

While we need not have recourse to Freud's help to explore the unconscious or subliminal world of the possessed, we must clearly recognize that the imagery and dramatization characteristic of the "demon's" assaults are simply the expression of a desire or a fear. This explains the regular association, in cases of this sort, of eroticism and fear of the pains of Hell, personified by the figure of the devil. We should properly add a second element: identification in suffering.

Magdalen of the Cross, prioress of the Poor Clares of Cordova, did not shrink from self-crucifixion in order to identify herself with our Lord, just as she imagined, in the light of a disordered imagination, a state of diabolical pregnancy, all the more impressive in that it began on the Annunciation and ended at Christmas.

With Sr. Jeanne of the Angels, the neurotic pregnancy may be considered the consequence of her incessant interviews with the unfortunate exorcist, who strove to expel from her body and soul the seven demons that had entered into her, some of which were, in Leon Bloy's words, "terrible gallants." Sr. Jeanne, the victim of her imagination, found herself at an impasse. How could she escape from this situation as a pregnant woman, after so positively stating and confirming it? Like those hysterical patients who get rid of a symptom which has become inconvenient, she took advantage of a great public exorcism to confound the doctor who had believed in her pregnancy and to astonish the public, for the demon "was compelled to make me bring up through my mouth all the mass of blood he had accumulated in my body."

Paroxysmal Forms of Pseudo-Diabolical Possession

*The Psycho-Physiological Structure
of the Hysterical Neurosis*

To specify these morbid states, of which examples have been given, I have appealed to the notion of neurosis or, rather, of psychoneurosis, and I have made use of the word *hysteria*.

But what is hysteria? Is it not just a myth, a collection of disparate and heterogeneous phenomena, which has never been defined, for the simple reason that the greater proportion of the manifestations of what was called, under Charcot, "the major neurosis" is only illusion and simulation?

As I have reminded readers, contrary to an opinion too widely held, even in medical circles unconnected with neurology, hysteria is very far from dead. Many examples of it are observed in our time, and although they are perhaps less spectacular than in the hectic days of the Salpêtrière, that is because we now understand better the inner nature of the neurosis and make use of better means to confine its manifestations and disperse them quickly.[38]

Admittedly, hysteria cannot be regarded as an illness in the strict sense of the word, like tuberculosis, typhoid, or some organic malady, such as the word *illness* suggests. Hysteria must not be envisaged in the abstract but, like life itself, in the concrete. What the neurologist observes is simply an aggregation of symptoms and particular reactions experienced by a particular

---

[38]There may also be social and cultural factors that disincline mentally disturbed individuals from manifesting this disturbance by means of unconsciously motivated hysterical behaviors. Studies in cross-cultural psychiatry suggest that psychopathology, which is universal and ubiquitous, can take different behavioral forms in different cultural and historical contexts. —Ed.

person placed in certain conditions. Briefly, the symptoms we call hysterical correspond with a definite psychosomatic state, which may remain latent during a long life and be brought into the light of day only by social disturbances.

Hysterical reactions are of an order that is social, ideological, or of the family; to be produced they require a certain moral climate and social setting. Isolated on an island like Robinson Crusoe's, neurotic hysterical reactions would be inconceivable. And it is precisely to the great social upheaval, in the storm which burst on the western world during 1914 to 1918, that we owe, indisputably, the recrudescence or the revival of that "major hysteria" which had remained hidden during the days of political and religious peace.

The scale of this work does not admit of an exhaustive study of the hysterical psychoneurosis, for that would require too long an elaboration. We need only say that hysterical reactions, however diverse they may appear to observation, respond to a particular structure.

Generally speaking, hysterical phenomena indicate a frail psychological organism, which is usually weak in the field of self-criticism and judgment. Experience of the World War of 1914-1918, in which France played such a considerable part, showed us that the patients subject to hysterical attacks or symptoms belonged to the least-educated social classes. When Henri Claude and I drew up the results of our very numerous observations, we came to the conclusion that, while hysterical manifestations were frequent among farmers, peasants, and country people, they never came to our notice among officers and doctors, although among both these classes cases of pretense were sometimes detected. Hysterical reactions, in fact, respond to a primitive mentality which has not reached the stage of criticism, and that is why history shows us that these phenomena are frequent in all ages, even the remotest of our civilization.

Thus the symptoms of the psychoneurosis correspond with a regression toward the infantile stage of the moral personality, with a dissociation of the psychological elements which should hold it together. One idea or sentiment predominates, and this seems to extinguish the other constituents of the psyche. One part of the personality escapes from the control of criticism and seems to be no longer attached to the self. It is this fairly simple mechanism that produces paralyses, contractures, spasms, grotesque and often very uncomfortable attitudes, which the patients sometimes keep up for years if treatment is not given in time. In this way, also, arise those sensitive-sensorial disorders, which are so common that they have often been considered the real hallmarks of the neurosis: anesthesia, analgesia, deafness, or blindness.

It is an odd fact, but the hysterical patient never complains of some serious symptom or other which must be making him suffer: he never goes to the doctor to ask advice or help. Indifferent, he seems to have lost the sense of a function, whether sensitive, sensorial, motor, or even visceral.[39] But if some serious incident occurs, which might threaten the safety of his life, the patient suddenly recovers the vanished function, thus giving to unlearned minds the impression of a miracle.

What has really happened? The primordial instinct of self-preservation has come into play, destroying in a moment all the fragile constructions of an unregulated imagination. As

---

[39]Here we mean disorders of the bladder, the intestines, or the stomach (mental anorexia of hysterical type).

all observers of the psychoneurosis have clearly noted, the fundamental element of hysteria responds to an elementary imaginative process, released by suggestion. Whether it is heterosuggestion or autosuggestion, the result is the same; the disjunction of one part of the personality, the escape of a physiological function from control. As Pierre Janet emphasized at length, hysterical manifestations always bear the mark of psychological insufficiency, of retreat from the field of consciousness, of reduction of the mental synthesis, so that a division is set up, a schism in the personality, which may lead to a genuine illness, and this, by its progressive evolution, will result in a psychological collapse: schizophrenia (Bleuler) or *dementia praecox* (Kraepelin). I ought here to remark that many pseudo-demoniacs who have come under my observation have fallen sooner or later into schizophrenia.

Hysteria could then be considered as a "schizosis," that is, a psychological affection with psychosomatic characteristics, determined by the dissociation of the self or of the conscious personality. This also suggests the considerable role played by the subconscious psyche in determining the accidents of hysteria, and the great importance for our problem of the discoveries of Sigmund Freud.

In the last analysis, as Charcot wrote about the works of his collaborator Pierre Janet, "these studies simply confirm a thought expressed in our lectures, that hysteria is very largely a mental illness." The term *mental illness* is perhaps too strong; nowadays we would prefer to call it an illness generating psychosomatic processes, insinuating itself into a psyche that is frail and particularly sensitive to all suggestions, whether these come from outside or derive their origin from subconscious or unconscious factors that many people have within them. These may be unknown or virtual, but catastrophes or some favorable moral climate can bring them up into light, to the astonishment of others who are insufficiently informed.

To these considerations we must add some reflections more peculiar to our subject. To many theologians the application of the term *hysteria* leads to a disparaging interpretation of the facts. And although the ancient idea of hysteria-neurosis engendered by Eros is abandoned, the fact remains that the hysterical subject is considered a simulator, a "supersimulator," according to the expression current during the first great war.

On a superficial examination, no doubt, it might appear that anybody could reproduce all the symptoms of hysteria, provided he wished to. But this is not the case. The symptoms of hysteria, whether they be the major convulsive attacks, paralyses, contractures, or anesthesia, cannot now be held to be artificial, that is, the products of a willingly consented simulation. It is impossible for a normal subject to reproduce them completely in their total reality and permanence.

We are not unaware, however, that the reactions proper to hysteria may be accompanied by a special psychological state that has been brought to light by the great psychiatrist Ernest Dupré and is called *mythomania,* the tendency to make believe, to the creation of untrue romances and lying statements. Already, in his lectures, Charcot had denounced the tendency of hysterical patients to duplicity, which shows that only a specially critical and informed mind is capable of detecting fraud among the genuine phenomena of the psychoneurosis. But this granted, it must certainly be said that, on the one hand, mythomania corresponds to a pathological state and not to deliberate falsehood and, on the other hand, that the most certainly hysterical symptoms can coexist with the highest virtues and a life worthy of admiration and respect, as the life of Marie-Thérèse Noblet, among others, bears witness.

Hysterical patients, like all other sick people, deserve our understanding and our charity.

Chapter 3

The Lucid Form of
Pseudo-Diabolical Possession

In the preceding chapters I have explained the different aspects under which paroxysmal or cataclysmal possessions appear. The normal personality here alternates with that of the "demon"; one takes the place of the other, although they are not unaware of each other, or else how could the possessed person think that an alien being is showing itself in him? As I have mentioned, however, there are cases in which the possessed seems to be invested simultaneously with two personalities, the normal and the demoniacal. But this is only an illusion, and patients of this type behave exactly like actors who soliloquize before an astounded audience.

In the form now to be described, the demoniacal control is permanent. While they speak to you, these patients have no doubt that they are penetrated by the evil spirit. So in the same mind there coexist two personalities who hate and fight each other bitterly.

It has been my lot to observe several cases that reveal this false possession, and I have tried to show that the psychological mechanism active in cases of this sort proves to be of exactly the same kind as that which the psychiatrist discovers at the source of pathological mental automatism.[40]

I can give a striking example of this. A man of about sixty, for many years a civil servant in one of the ministries, came to consult me on the advice of an exorcist who had at once guessed the nature of his disease. This man, whose *external* conduct was unimpeachable, told me that for a long time past he had felt himself to be manipulated, possessed by the demon. This diabolical control was something of which he was absolutely convinced. To begin with, he heard sounding in himself "offensive, substantial, and filthy words." "Ironical thoughts came to his mind, applying to the most respectable persons." Soon the devil threatened him: "If you advance, you are dead," Satan said to him. "I shall summon all the legions of Hell against you." Later, the devil caused him to see scenes of perverse immorality, the more repugnant because he was forced to witness persons "in postures of homosexuality or connected with nymphomania."

Everything around him became a pretext for symbolization. The devil stayed near him in image, at the same time gliding into his inner self to reveal or recall things which horrified him. This influence of the evil spirit left him no respite, while it entailed a constant restraint over his thoughts and actions. Dialogues took place between the demon within him and his own personality, in the course of which the devil was irritated if he opposed, mocked, or threatened him.

My patient, a man of great intelligence, explained to me how, if he resisted by taking refuge in silence, the devil would formulate in succession both questions and answers. More than that, it provoked a sort of automatic language. "Words formed

---

[40]See Lhermitte, *Mystiques et faux mystiques*.

themselves on his lips without the consent of his own will, giving an impression of spurious possession." And in this inner conflict against the diabolical control my patient got to the point of wondering whether the devil, so cunning and subtle, was not trying to make him believe in a real possession. Could not the feeling of domination he experienced be compared to a sort of induced current? However that might be, he was certain that the evil spirit made him think, feel, and act in a manner repugnant to him, striving to bring about "a rupture of union, of thought and heart, with the powers he invoked," meaning, of course, the celestial powers.

But it must not be supposed that the devil confined itself to acting on his mind, thoughts, and feelings; it influenced and regulated his physiological behavior. Thus, the patient would suddenly feel an irresistible desire to sleep, while "with his lips he rejected the malign internal whisper." In addition, there were "attacks on the head, the optic nerve, and the pineal gland" and, one suspects, the genital organs, in a frequent state of "nervous excitement" or "emotion." As I was given to understand, the man tried by every possible means, physical, psychological, and spiritual, to combat the demoniacal influence. In what he called his "mental defenses" he included silence, self-exorcism, prayer to the archangel Michael and recourse to three powers, St. Teresa of Avila, St. Thérèse of the Child Jesus, and our Blessed Lady.

With a little attention, the "possessed" man continues, "the division takes place, one sees nothing more. Everything happens as if the evil spirit were arrested and forbidden to persevere. Above all, one must never compromise."

I have here reported only some of the more expressive marks of the psychosis with which this possessed man was afflicted, but the remarkable thing is the result of the autoanalysis to which the man abandoned himself. From all the evidence, he did not doubt that the devil acted on him in all sorts of ways, making him experience repugnant sentiments, to think and act against his will and in opposition to his true self. But, he asked himself, am I really possessed by the devil; is it not trying to impose on me the conviction of a possession which is not real? "Certainly," he wrote, "I am the victim of the devil's malice at the same time as I am benefiting from the support of the divine powers." But, after all, in what manner can the evil spirit act? By influencing my thoughts, by distorting my actions, by suspending a part of my social activity, by making me hear locutions which are abject, ignoble, obscene, etc. All this I can well understand, but might not the devil have a still more subtle mode of action? I mean, not by unhinging or disowning my brain, but by producing the semblance of a psychoneurosis."

It should be noticed that the subject never in any way envisages being attacked by a mental affliction; he only wonders whether the repeated diagnosis of his state as psychoneurosis is not in reality a delusive appearance created by the cunning, the hypocritical ruse of the evil spirit.

The case I have recorded is far from exceptional, and I have observed others like it. But I have studied it in such detail because it here appears in its "pure state," so to speak, and enables us to understand the tragic series of events of which Fr. Surin was the victim at Loudun.

The Case of Fr. Surin

The strange behavior of this great mystic, the exorcist of Sr. Jeanne of the Angels, was the subject of many commentaries, and many attempts have been made to diagnose the remarkable psychological anomaly of the author of the *Spiritual Catechism* and the *Spiritual Dialogues*.[41]

Exactly as with the patient I have been describing, the very obvious disorder in the psychological sphere did not weaken his higher functions, and it cannot be too often emphasized that it was at the end of his life that Fr. Surin wrote his finest works. We are faced, then, with a mystery rather similar to that which still surrounds the personality of Hamlet. Was Fr. Surin a lunatic or a man possessed by the devil?

Without question, from the day Fr. Surin assumed the functions of exorcist to Jeanne of the Angels, his life began to abound in singularities. It is equally obvious that no temperament could have been less suited to this role than that of this Jesuit Father, transported into a world that was feverish and profoundly disturbed by the growing number of possessed persons, whose nervous state, writes Fr. Poulain, was spreading like an infectious disease.[42]

"All the churches of Loudun," confessed Fr. Surin, "were occupied by the exorcists, and a prodigious crowd of people watched what was happening: there was not one who was not obsessed, and I myself was the very first."

[41] See Bremond, *Histoire littéraire du sentiment religieux en France*; R.P. Olphe Gaillard, "Le Père Surin et les Jésuites de son temps," *Études Carmélitaines: Sainteté et Folie* (October 1938): 177; P. Joseph de Guibert, "Le cas du Père Surin," in *Études Carmélitaines* (October 1938): 183; E. de Greeff, "Le cas du Père Surin," in *Études Carmélitaines* (October 1938): 152; Gelma, "La psychopathie melancolique du Père Surin," in *Cahiers de Psychiatrie*, no. 1 (1951); Lhermitte, *Mystiques et faux mystiques*, 197.

[42] A. Poulain, *Graces of Interior Prayer* (London, 1950), 433, footnote.

It is therefore not surprising to learn from Fr. Surin himself that he was "assailed by temptations to such appalling impurities that without a miraculous grace he could never have defended himself." But, despite his every effort to escape the power of the demon, he was obliged to succumb to it. Not only did the devil publicly possess him, a minister of the Church, but again when "Leviathan," at his command, left Sr. Jeanne's body, it entered his own. "Then the Mother became very calm, and I ceased to be so."

In spite of the strangeness of the phenomena and their danger, the exorcisms of Sr. Jeanne continued. And in 1635, when Fr. Surin was thirty-five years old, all those symptoms appeared which I witnessed in that girl whose tragic trials I reported. The demon that possessed him was chiefly that of impurity: it provoked in him sensations and "natural representations" of such violence that "the temptation almost drove him mad."

The wretched Fr. Surin could not help persuading himself that it was no longer he who ruled his conduct, but a detestable being inside him, commanding his ideas and actions, for every day the devils were active in the bodies of most of the Ursulines, and Sr. Jeanne, his penitent, confided to him her most tender "ravishments," at the same time aping that demoniacal display which was most likely to overexcite the imagination.

Very soon, it seems, the idea of diabolical influence invaded Fr. Surin's mind, so as to transform or confirm it in the conviction that he was possessed. He describes the mechanism of this state as he understands it. Writing to a friend in the Society of Jesus, he says:

I cannot explain what happens within me, and how this spirit (the evil one) unites himself with me without depriving me either of my liberty or of my consciousness. He becomes, nonetheless, like another self; it is then as if I had two souls, one of which is deprived of the use of its bodily organs and remains afar off, watching the actions of the one which has taken possession of the body, while this other acts in the body as if it were its master. I feel that the spirit of God and the spirit of the demon are using my body and soul as a battlefield, and each makes his own impressions on it. On the demon's part, they are of rage and aversion from God, giving me an impetuous desire to be separated from him forever; and at the same time I experience a great sweetness, profound peace, heavenly joy.

I feel the state of damnation and apprehend it and this stranger soul which seems to be mine is penetrated with despair as though by arrows, while the other soul, which is full of faith, despises these impressions and freely curses him who causes them; indeed, I feel that the same cries which escape my lips come equally from these two souls, and I am at pains to tell whether they are produced by joy or by the extreme madness which fills me.

Inspired by two such opposed principles, Fr. Surin could not fail to be very singular in his behavior, so he was judged by his fellow-Jesuits to be *infirmus* and even placed under supervision at Saint-Macaire. On this point again, this man who was so "obsessed"[43] with possession provides us with the most explicit details. He writes: "If, at the intervention of one of these souls, I wish to make the Sign of the Cross on my lips, the other

---

[43] The term *obsessed* is used in its theological, not in its medical, sense.

forcibly snatches my hand away and seizes my finger with my teeth to bite me with fury."

We need not, I think, dwell on the very numerous psychical and psychosensory hallucinations from which Fr. Surin suffered, for these were very similar to those of my former patient. What is chiefly important in either case is the profound sense of a division of the personality into two halves, one of which the subject attributes to himself and is what he would wish to be, while the other is that which possesses him in spite of himself, which constrains and directs him, and from which he longs at any price to be free.

I could report many other personal observations, but Christian discretion obliges me not to publish them.

Nonetheless, one feels a very natural astonishment at the preservation of the intellectual functions in cases of this sort. I will briefly mention what I observed in a patient over a period of more than ten years, a man who likewise believed he was possessed by the devil. Like Surin, he had begun by feeling that a force was being exerted over him, then the impression of constraint became more vivid, and soon he persuaded himself that the devil was inside him, acting on his physical and moral personality. In this man, the devil was not felt or conceived merely as the evil spirit; it was materialized. The patient felt it in his body; more than that, he used to vomit it or spit it out, and when the devil went out of his mouth he felt burning or a taste of sulfur on his lips, or the pain of claws or nails scratching his lips.

Now in spite of such a well-established, deeply rooted delirium, and in spite of this split of the personality, this patient always retained a lively intelligence and appeared able, without anyone noticing anything strange, to carry on uninterruptedly a brilliant course of teaching.

The Lucid Form of Pseudo-Diabolical Possession

The Psychological Structure
of Lucid Possession

The facts I have sketched oblige us now to face the question of the mechanism that regulates and determines this type of "pseudo-demoniacal possession."

For there to be an appearance of possession, the subject must experience the feeling of being constrained in both thought and action by a power stronger than himself; he must feel himself both "possessed" by a power and "dispossessed of his liberty." This is precisely the feeling and the idea we find expounded in the writings of Fr. Surin and in the notebooks written by my patient, whose sad story I have recorded. Neither hesitates to conclude that his being is shared between two personalities. Is it then possible to hold that the self can ever be divided by a pathological process? To the theologian, Oesterreich says, "the reality of an inner division in the state of possession is clearly evident," and he quotes Harnack: "The patient's consciousness, as he professes, his will and sphere of activity are duplicated:... he has the impression that there is within him a second being which dominates and governs him. He thinks, feels, and acts now as the one, now as the other, and with the conviction that he is dual." It could not be better expressed.

But must we conclude that the self is really divided? Are we not in the presence of an illusion? Oesterreich very pertinently remarks that on this hypothesis we must either believe in the conditioned appearance of a new subject, bearing no relation at all to the first, the normal one, or else in a real division of the first subject, the real self. However, he continues, "if there is division of the subject, we have therefore two series of psychic processes: the one belongs to the one subject, the other to the other. Neither of the two possesses an immediate knowledge of the other." And later he says: "If the subject is something absolute, not only from the point of view of functions or composition, but as constituting a unity in itself and for itself, its division is in every way impossible, particularly if it must be effected without change."

This philosophical argument is based on strict logic, and it is certain that two absolutely pure "selves" cannot coexist in our "possessed" patients. But granting this, we are bound to defer to what is asserted by all our subjects, who feel in themselves a dual center of thoughts and feelings, and a dual source of activity. As a "possessed" patient studied by L. and J. Gayral says: "My being seems to me to be cut in two: the being who judges and has love and respect for everyone, and the being who is judged and is gradually degraded."[44]

Pierre Janet goes further, although he does not completely resolve the difficulty. "Man is subject to subconscious dreams, produced by automatic acts; if the mind is weakened, these automatic dreams develop and become defined, then involuntary, and soon there is duplication. The patient attributes his trouble to one influence or another and, in some cases, to the devil."

St. John of the Cross, in his critical analysis of the imaginary or successive words so common with certain mystics, proved even shrewder in denouncing the facility with which the man who retreats into himself and indulges in contemplation can imagine that he is not the author of the words he hears interiorly and persuades himself that "it is another person who forms these reasonings within himself."

[44]L. Gayral and J. Gayral, *Les délires de possession diabolique* (Paris: Vigot, 1944).

The Lucid Form of Pseudo-Diabolical Possession

Under the influence of subconscious feelings and the pressure of cenesthetic disturbances, the mind may then be capable of creating a system of thoughts and affective elements which, because of their affinity and common origin in the depths of the subconscious, unite to form a complex whole, of which the subject, although unconsciously, is the creator, and which appears to be a dual personality.

In reality, the self cannot be duplicated, divided, or split, but it can experience the illusion of it, because this second personality seems either to have a divine appearance, as with the false mystics, or to be so opposed to what the subject desires to be that he can only imagine it to be diabolical.

We should note that this apparent splitting is not peculiar to pseudo-mystics or "possessed" persons, but appears very obviously in many who suffer from persecution mania or similar afflictions, as well as in spiritualists in trance. The patient presented by G. de Clerambault, at the beginning of his clinical researches into mental automatism, clearly displayed this mechanism. This woman, who was not haunted by any religious ideas, declared that "she was given ideas which were not her own; that there arose in her mind depressions or absurdities, of which she could not discover the source." This mysterious power that possessed her, "which disorganized her brain": what could it be? Perhaps some discarnate spirit, she thought. It is rather remarkable, by the way, that possession by "spirits" has increased in proportion with the modern growth of the so-called science of spiritualism and has multiplied the more as demonopathic possession has decreased.

But to return to the problem of "dual personality." According to de Clerambault, there is a group of psychopathies that are based on the splitting of the personality, so that the subject has the illusion that he is formed of two entities, different and utterly opposed; one in which he recognizes himself, the other which he energetically repudiates. The personality "Primus," in de Clerambault's terminology, wants to be the social personality, the one the subject has constructed for himself; the personality "Secundus"—sprung, I repeat, from the subconscious activity—provides the subject with information on what is going on in the deepest region of the psyche, the intellectual and affective subconscious. But the Secundus, which is often revealed to be megalomanic, sarcastic, pestering, hypersexual, or perverted, provokes an often violent reaction on the part of the Primus, who tries by every possible means to correct the faults of the Secundus, so as to impose its law on it. Now this throwback can only rebound on the Secundus, which retorts with insults or sarcasms, and so there are interminable soliloquies and exhausting vicious circles.

Accordingly, while there is no real division of the self, the self seems to be faced with an illusive, artificial personality, which it has itself constructed, but does not recognize. And when the Christian patient is filled with the fear or horror of "bad thoughts," he easily slips from the scruple of obsession to the delirium of possession, by materializing in the diabolical being the representations, feelings, and tendencies which he detests and wishes at all costs to reject.

The subject of false demoniacal possession is too vast for me to pretend to have given a complete picture of such a complex state; I have merely tried to define the most striking features of the two fundamental types of this affliction: the cataclysmal or intermittent and the lucid or continuous. The reader will easily understand that these two types do not in themselves constitute illnesses, but simply syndromes; these may figure as component elements in a great number of mental illnesses, which it is the task of the psychiatrist to differentiate.

And since the "possessions" I have envisaged correspond to natural psychophysiological mechanisms, the doctor must not find himself defenseless against these manifestations. From the preventive point of view, he must beware of any ill-advised suggestion, for imaginary possession is one of the most easily induced maladies. Exorcism, "that dangerous ministry," must never become an ill-considered or imprudent practice,[45] and it must be remembered that if one calls up the devil, one will see, not the devil himself, but a portrait composed according to the patient's idea of him.[46]

Antoine Gay, the Possessed Worshipper

As the Gospel stories clearly show, neither the demons nor Satan their master are in the habit, when they take possession of a man, of making him say prayers or inciting him to pronounce thanksgivings and even to praise God or our Lady. The story of a historical character, Antoine Gay, who believed himself to be possessed, therefore deserves some consideration.[47]

Born on May 31, 1790, in the Ain department, Antoine Gay had a rudimentary education and learned the trade of a joiner.

---

[45] F. X. Macquart, *Études Carmélitaines, Satan* (1948), 328, English trans., 178.

[46] R. P. de Tonquédec, *Les maladies nerveuses et mentales et les manifestations diaboliques* (Paris, Beauchesne, 1938).

[47] The extraordinary story of Antoine Gay is told in detail in the book by J. H. Gruninger, *Le possédé qui glorifia la Sainte Vierge* (Lyons, 1954). Cf. also Nicolas Corte, *Who Is the Devil?* (Manchester, New Hampshire: Sophia Institute Press, 2013), 118-126.

In about his thirtieth year he made a vow to enter religion and even received the habit of a lay brother. But soon, troubled with a nervous affliction, he was unable to satisfy the demands of the monastic life. Exactly what the nervous disorder that prevented him from following the rule was we do not know, although this may be guessed in the course of his story.

At the age of forty-seven Antoine appeared to show indubitable signs of possession, and thereafter the trouble only increased. Three demons, writes M. Gruninger, had taken up their abode in his body: Isacaron, prince of the demons of impurity, and two others, one of lying, the other of avarice, called "the dog" and "the wolf." Thus the possessed man "barked like a dog, howled like a wolf, and grunted like a pig."

Gay's friends, out of pity, sent him back to the Trappist monastery of Aiguebelle, provided with certificates from priests and doctors. Although, we are assured, the abbot was convinced that the possession was genuine, he did not consider it prudent or necessary to use exorcism and referred him to his friend, the chaplain of the Brothers at Privas. Gay stayed there for three weeks, but here too he was not subjected to any exorcism. The poor man then returned to Lyons to practice his trade as a joiner. But then the people became alarmed: was this gesticulating, abusive demoniac to be allowed at large, even if he were not actually dangerous?

Judged to be a lunatic, Gay was then admitted to Antiquaille, an old hospital in Lyons, where he remained for three months. When discharged, our "possessed" friend attracted the sympathy of two worthy priests who introduced him to Cardinal de Bonald, the archbishop of the diocese. But after reading a letter from Antoine, requesting the favor of an exorcism, the cardinal confined himself to giving a few words of consolation.

To mitigate this fresh disappointment, a priest, Fr. Marie-Joseph Chiron, decided to devote himself to comforting poor Antoine, who took the habit of the Third Order and became Br. Joseph-Marie. In 1853 Fr. Chiron accompanied him to the monastery of Vernet-les-Bains, still hoping to obtain the favor of an exorcism.

But note this: what led Fr. Chiron to go near Perpignan was not only his desire to obtain Antoine's deliverance from possession, but also his interest in a "possessed woman," mother of three children. "The whole parish had seen her running extremely fast, and nobody doubted the reality of a diabolic power, for she was raised about two feet above the ground."

Now while Fr. Chiron was in the house of this unfortunate woman, somebody brought him a young woman called Chiquette, thirty-six years old, who since the age of sixteen had been stricken by the demon with dumbness. But if Chiquette was incapable of speech, the demon inside her, which answered to the name of Modeste, was certainly not.

And so Chiquette and Antoine, thus brought together, lost no time in exteriorizing their "possession." The demons Modeste and Isacaron, we are told, were like mad dogs. "They spoke a language," wrote Fr. Chiron, "of which we understand nothing. They insulted and humiliated each other, and I was often obliged to intervene to prevent them coming to blows.... Apart from possession," he continues, "such things are inexplicable."

Returning to Lyons, Gay again begged for the favor of an exorcism, but in vain. Life at Lyons did not proceed without vexatious manifestations on his part, for "he was taken seven times to the preventive cell" at the Hôtel de Ville of Lyons and detained four times at the old prison called Roanne.

The unfortunate man's afflictions were indeed most painful. Isacaron inflicted on him not only atrocious bodily pains but also appalling moral tortures. As a fervent Christian, he desired with all his heart to perform his religious duties and by his humility, prayers, and devotions to obtain some relief from his martyrdom, but now the demon forbade him to attend the services of the Church or to go to confession. "You shall not confess till I have left your body. There has never been a possession like this, and there will never be another!" he whispered. Antoine became desperate at seeing that nothing could be done to relieve his afflictions. "The world is taking the demon's side," he wrote. Already we see a rather revealing mark of the persecution complex that gripped our poor hero, and this was still more accentuated by a matter of family inheritance. He thought that his sisters were trying to divert some family property to their own advantage and that the judges of the case had shown scandalous partiality.

The internal agitation tormenting this poor man did not fail to show itself in his strange behavior: children avoided him or jeered at him; he lived apart. At last, in spite of his appeals, and in spite of the efforts of the religious and priests who supported him, the exorcists refused their help and, on his deathbed, Antoine found it impossible to make his confession: Isacaron made him dumb. The evil spirit never ceased to repeat: "Not before exorcism."

Such, in brief outline, is the tragic story of a poor man whom some still hold to have been a genuine case of possession by the devil.

Alleged proofs are certainly not lacking: discernment of spirits, clairvoyance, premonitions, sight of the future, inexplicable cures, reading of people's hearts—"I know all the inhabitants of the earth," he declared emphatically—theological and linguistic knowledge: and these do not exhaust the list. But though we are swamped with the facts offered as proofs of the authenticity of the "possession," I would have preferred some substantial documentation, some observation carried out by qualified persons, and not simply by those who may have been very good men but were quite without psychological or medical competence.

If Antoine Gay could really have been considered a genuinely possessed man, how was it that the highest and most competent authorities of the Church always refused, in spite of the most urgent pleas, to apply the exorcism for which the wretched man so longed and which seemed the only remedy for a hopeless situation?

No; as those well informed and instructed in questions of demonopathy perfectly understood, Antoine was not genuinely possessed. His case is one of the category of "lucid delirious possession," of one suffering from paranoiac persecution mania, and of very weak critical intelligence.

The reason we have dealt with this case at such length is that in this unfortunate, divided against himself, Isacaron (as he thought) having gained hold of his personality, never ceased to praise God and the Blessed Virgin. The evil spirit, in truth, here appears in the guise of an "apostolic devil," which surely seems paradoxical enough. No doubt, as M. Gruninger writes, "it was only in self-defense that Isacaron filled this role, but he often did so, with a zeal which a holy missionary would not have disavowed, and a talent which many preachers would envy."

Sovereign Master, one only God in three Persons, Father, Son, and Holy Spirit, Creator of all things save sin, of which Satan is the inventor, God of goodness, wisdom, power, and infinite mercy, Thou art He who was before time, who is and ever shall be, of whom we demons are all the accursed slaves, and whom I, Isacaron, obey by force, against all Hell, to exclaim against the disorders which fill the world.

O God, infinitely great, infinitely holy, infinitely just, infinitely good, Thou dost not despise the most miserable of Thy creatures; what have I done to deserve the graces Thou givest me, unworthy as I am? Would I had tears of blood to bewail all my ingratitude and all the offenses I have had the misfortune to commit against Thee!

To hymn the glory of the holy Virgin "Isacaron becomes sublime," continues M. Gruninger. "No tongue can praise the Mother of God as she deserves: no creature can comprehend her greatness, her goodness, and her power. Mary alone has more strength than all the angels, all creatures, all the saints together. Those who refuse to believe in her virginity, her motherhood, her Immaculate Conception, will perish eternally."

I may be excused for not being struck with amazement at the productions of an alleged evil spirit, who only repeats, in an emphatic and grandiloquent fashion, all that has been said and written more soberly by the pastors, the preachers, and the authors of our catechisms.

Chapter 4

Witchcraft and Diabolical Possession

In our own days we scarcely ever come across sorcerers, but it was very different in the Middle Ages and even in the sixteenth and seventeenth centuries, and the history of sorcery or witchcraft throws much light on the subject of demoniacal possession.

In the first place, we must remember that the sorcerer is not to be confused with the magician. The magician acts on those who resort to him by using processes unknown to science and repugnant to it, but the devil is not necessarily involved. The sorcerer, on the contrary, is a person whose influence is exerted through the medium of the demon. Whether the evil spirit is invoked from without, as in external demonopathy, or from within, as in genuine demoniacal possession, the result is the same; it is always the supposed power of the demon that comes into action.

As M. Amadou rightly reminds us, if the sorcerer is genuinely possessed, he does not permanently remain so; on the other hand, he facilitates the intervention of the demon by prayers, invocations, incantations, and a whole set of "magic" means, even by material technical processes, such as fomentations or technical ointments. The sexual intercourse of the "possessed" which we observe in our days is wholly involuntary: the incubus and the succuba are both subjected to it, whereas wizard and witch invite it, desire it, share it, and approve it with all their hearts.

These are the essential characteristics of the sorcerer as distinct from the "possessed." In reality, we must admit that, while there is this delicate distinction between sorcerers and possessed, we cannot see any formal contradiction between these two modes of demonopathy. Equally it is not forbidden to look for a natural explanation of each of these modes, saving always, of course, our belief in the real influence of Satan in the world. We need not remind our readers that the Church has always taken the same attitude toward sorcerers who invoke the devil as toward those she considers to be genuinely possessed.

Granting these general principles, we can examine the singular manifestations that history attributes to the sorcerers, those henchmen of the devil. We shall not find them in works on psychology or mental medicine, but in the judicial records, for wizards or witches have been the chief figures in countless trials. We owe a debt of special gratitude to such an archivist as M. Étienne Delcambre,[48] who, with unwearying patience and absolute objectivity, has undertaken the task of expounding in detail the witchcraft trials that occurred in the duchy of Lorraine in the sixteenth and seventeenth centuries. I point out at once that the facts reported by this author are not peculiar to the history of this region; the same scenes were enacted before the tribunals of far distant provinces, and if we examine them

---

[48]Étienne Delcambre, *Les jeteurs de sort, noamment dans l'ancienne Lorraine* (Nancy: Société d'archéologie lorraine, 1950).

attentively we always find the same procedure, so that a single explanation can be valid for the witchcraft of Languedoc, of Poitou, and of Lorraine.

As I have mentioned, the sorcerer invokes the demon and asks for his help; more, he tries to be united to him, so that it has been said that witchcraft is simply "an inverted mysticism," That is why some theologians have depicted it like a diptych: the divine mysticism and the diabolical. So we need not be surprised that the behavior of the sorcerer resembles some of the points that strike us in some false mystics. Imaginary or corporeal visions, auditions, the feeling of being influenced, the apparent splitting of the personality, are found in the sorcerers as well as in the "possessed" demoniacs. This fact is of considerable importance, for it allows us to suppose that one and the same element is to be found at the root of witchcraft and at that of the false possessions, and that is what we must now try to discover.

We know how powerfully and earnestly the great Christian mystics—St. John of the Cross, St. Teresa of Jesus, and others, not to mention the pure mystics of the Eastern Churches—have taught that we must refuse to accept everything presented to us by the senses. Now with the sorcerer, the pretended influence of the demon relies precisely on so-called corporeal phenomena. While the sentiment of an immaterial presence is common with the mystic, and the feeling of an influence often haunts the "possessed," the mind of the sorcerer is peopled with phenomena which are purely corporeal, that is, palpable to the senses. The demon is not felt as an "evil spirit," but shows itself under the most hideous and always repugnant forms; a feline or canine appearance, horrible to behold, infesting the atmosphere with a nauseous stench.

True or False Possession?

In the case of a witch, the devil visits her in the form of a goat, a howling wolf, a terrifying bull, a rat, a hare, a snake, a lizard, or even beasts impossible to identify, but grossly obvious in their symbolic significance. With the wizard, the diabolical forms resemble those of a woman, either under the aspect of a perverted or alluring Eve, or in the guise of caressing animals, or of mobile shadows subject to strange metamorphoses, or of mysterious fire, mobile and blue (Delcambre).

Generally the corporeal visions are not seen by the sorcerer's companions, although this rule has its exceptions which, as we may guess, greatly increase the credibility accorded to the satanic apparitions. But these apparitions, often accompanied by foul smells, seem to the sorcerer a strong proof of the presence of the evil one. Further, the proof of the devil's reality is revealed, it seems, by the accompaniment of audible words.

The diabolical apparitions are not only apparent to sight and smell; there are some that whisper, speak into the ear, or howl. Thus, Nicolas Remy reports, when Satan desires to transmit a secret message to one of his servants, he changes himself into a little fly that murmurs in his ear.[49]

No doubt the demon can be clever at disguise and hide its presence under the form of an animal of normal appearance, but it is recognized by "the absence of a tail."[50] It is interesting to observe that certain possessed persons in our own day, haunted by visits from the demon, declare that it most often appears in a human form but betrays itself "by the lack of a tail"

---

[49]Delcambre, *Les jeteurs de sort, noamment dans l'ancienne Lorraine*, 178.

[50]See Jean Lhermitte, "Les pseudo-possessions démoniaques, séquelles d'encéphalite épidémique," *Bull. de l'Académie de Médecine* (1955).

and also by its disappearing when sprinkled with holy water or exposed to some "sacramental," such as the Sign of the Cross.

In time of trial and especially in imprisonment, the demon's visits become more frequent and painful. Its influence over the prisoner is such that the latter can transport himself in spirit to another place, crossing the walls of the prison, to visit distant persons and places. It was by such a satanic intervention, Delcambre reports, that the magistrates of Charmes explained the apparition of a witch: the demon, in the judges' opinion, must have transported her in ecstasy outside the prison. How else could it be explained, they said, "that being a prisoner in this castle, she can see a woman who is in her home or elsewhere"? The hypothesis of a dream or rapture in spirit being discarded, the fact of a bodily transporting seemed to the magistrates the only plausible explanation of such an appearance in such a place.

It is noteworthy that the visits of the demon to the prison where the witches are incarcerated do not always bring fear, sadness, or affliction. More than once, we are told, the devil cheers his servant with the hope of a speedy release if the secret is well kept. In case the accused has already started to make confessions, he compels her to retract and persuades her that by such a disavowal she will escape the clutches of the law. The devil's attentions may include cheering the unfortunate women with his bodily presence or even having carnal intercourse with them.

Stubborn in his decisions and his control over his henchmen, the demon accompanies his slaves to the dock and during the torture. According to Nicolas Remy, Satan is more assiduous than ever and does not hesitate to appear to his slaves in the very sanctum of justice, among the bench of judges. Belief in Satan's personification is so deep that Remy is astonished at not being able to see him, when a prisoner pointed him out with his finger, and the worthy man is convinced that he himself was the object of a diabolic enchantment, preventing him from seeing Satan, who was visible only to his servants.

With great good sense, Étienne Delcambre considers that the myth of internal visions, in all periods, arises from a pathological deviation of the mental functions, whether it is a case of obsession, of persecution mania or of simple hysteria, and that all the strange phenomena we have reported can only have been aggravated during the imprisonment and the trial and during the pangs of torture. The author adds that "in this field, mystical theology has exerted a definite influence." Clarifying his thought, Delcambre is careful to add that the supposedly satanic phenomena reproduce only the lowest, as it were material, form of the mystical experience. Between certain visions of a St. Teresa of Jesus or a St. John of the Cross and those claimed to have been seen by the vampires of Lorraine and the west, we find a difference not only of content but also of nature. So then, the wizard appears as essentially subordinated to the demon's pleasure; worse, he becomes the slave of an inexorable master, a mysterious creature whose yoke is as burdensome as that of Christ is light.

A witch of Brouvelieures declares that "since she gave herself to the demon, instead of receiving any courtesy, nothing but ill fortune and poverty has befallen her."

On the pattern of the "possessed," the wizard receives from his master imperative orders, forbidding him to pray to God, to implore God's help, to go to church, and especially to put his trust in the Almighty by prayer and charity. Forbidden, too, are the sacramentals and the sacraments and, above all, the Blessed

Sacrament. But—a very peculiar point—it is not so much the idea of bad dispositions in the soul which haunts the wizard as the material profanation of the eucharistic Body. That is why amateurs of satanism, beginning with Huysmans in *Là-Bas*, have delighted to describe Black Masses, sacrileges, and profanations under realistic colors, which are, incidentally, the most suited to the resources of an art that considers itself naturalistic.

Satan threatens, commands his slaves imperiously, obliges them to do evil, to eschew all that comes from God, and therefore, sometimes, to kill their neighbors or destroy themselves. Thus the demon orders a wizard of Paire in Moyenmoutier to kill his own wife (Delcambre); the wretch refuses and is tempted to suicide. An accused woman at Étiral is given the formal injunction to kill her husband; refusing this order, the poor woman pays for her disobedience with a long illness. Some of those vampires who had refused to obey the orders of the fiend were beaten until their bodies were covered with bruises.

Sometimes it is not only by a kind of intuition that the vampire or wizard is invited to commit suicide or murder; the order is conveyed by a voice which cries: "Kill yourself, kill yourself!" or "Kill him, kill him!"

Nowadays we can observe absolutely identical phenomena in our cases of possession. One of my patients, for example, during a state of depression heard the devil in the middle of the night speaking to her and bidding her kill her child, then a few months old. The woman, whose child slept beside her, was horrified and indignant and for several nights merely told her husband the orders the demon had bidden her carry out. But one night she suddenly woke up in a state of anxiety; the demon whispered in her ear: "Kill it, then, kill it!" After a few short moments of resistance, the poor woman got up, took her child in its cradle, and threw it out of the window from the second floor. A good guardian angel, no doubt, intervened; the child was bruised but not killed. As for the mother, when she had been given electric shock treatment,[51] she was not long in recovering her mental equilibrium.

The facts, of which I have given the most essential traits, show that in principle the vampires and sorcerers who are the devil's slaves have sought his assistance voluntarily, while the "possessed" are forced to endure the moral tortures of the evil one and beg to be delivered from his power. But they also show that in actual fact there is only a frail barrier between these two classes of slaves to the devil's power.

From the social, prophylactic, and therapeutic points of view (setting aside certain exceptional cases), sorcerers and the possessed require the same treatment.

---

[51] This procedure, still used in psychiatry with the aid of anesthesia, is now known as "electroconvulsive therapy," or ECT. — Ed

Chapter 5

Some Modern Ideas on Demonopathic Possession

Whether we like it or not, the introduction of Freudian psychoanalysis into contemporary thought has spread, in the last few decades, to all sectors in which the mind is especially concerned. And if one can no longer imagine any literary or artistic criticism, biography or hagiography, without references to the doctrine of the Sage of Vienna, one need not be surprised to learn that not even the devil has escaped the clutches of the psychoanalyst.[52]

The capture, we must say, was very easy and therefore very tempting. We know that for believers in the Freudian doctrine it is necessary to carry out investigations in depth into the earliest steps of the psychological life of the child, if we are to begin to grasp the development and birth of the psychopathic disturbances of the adult.

Accordingly, since the first psychological analyses began, many philosophers have insisted that the human soul is not simple and that while it contains noble or sublime tendencies,

---

[52]Rosette Dubal, *La Psychanalyse du Diable* (Paris: Corréa, 1953).

it is not without instinctive urges, the repression of which demands more suppleness and penetration than many parents and teachers possess.

Our personality, our total self, is then composed of an equilibrium of opposing forces: those of the instincts and those which form what the analysts call the superego. What is this, at bottom, but the collection of moral rules imposed by society and religion?

It is obvious that this superego must be opposed to the urges of instinct, which desires only pleasure and has no concern for social restrictions or the laws promulgated by morality. So this superego, which can only repeat: "You must" or "You must not," appears as a troubler, a persecutor of the person, thus divided against itself. *Video meliora proboque, deteriora sequor*,[53] Ovid confessed, and Racine says: *Mon Dieu, quelle guerre cruelle, je sens deux hommes en moi.*[54] Thus man becomes the scene of the duel between God and the devil, the debate between what ought to be and what is.

From this conflict springs an anguish, exhausting and insatiable, impelling the subject to eject this superego which opposes his libidinal aspirations and leading him to give it the form of the devil. The sentiment of guilt, the weight of a conscience judging itself guilty—that, according to the psychoanalysts, is the source of the demoniacal illusion. We may go further: Mme. Rosette Dubal recalls the judgment of Freud: "The devil is nothing but the incarnation of the repressed anal impulses."

We refrain from exploring Freud's teaching on this point and only note that, from the psychoanalytic point of view, to

[53] I see the better and approve it: I follow the worse.
[54] O God, what a cruel war is this! I feel two men within me.

repel or repress the instinctive desires, which are part of the forces of our ego, is useless, for the demon is within us and its repression often only succeeds in reinforcing its power.

If we are to believe Mme. Dubal, it seems that hysteria and schizophrenia correspond most closely to the psychical disorders entailed by the struggle of the self against the superego, which overpowers and enslaves it. The conflict induced by schizophrenia appears to be rather of the criminal than the sexual order; the "double" has not the face of Eros but of the diabolical superego; the ego can therefore only strive to cast it into outer darkness.

We can clearly see that in all its stages, in the very structure of its doctrine, psychoanalysis leads us into the paths of animism: "The greatest power ever given to men is to give a soul to things which have none" (Napoleon).

But really, if we jettison all the frail imaginative construction it contains, the doctrine of psychoanalysis strikes an already familiar note. The great Christian mystics, beginning with St. Teresa of Jesus and St. John of the Cross, had perfectly divined the psychological mechanism of those deviations of the mind that imagined duplication of the personality, which is mere illusion. St. John of the Cross writes: "I am appalled at what happens in these days—namely, when a soul with the very smallest experience of meditation, if it be conscious of certain locutions of this kind in some state of recollection, at once christens them all as coming from God, and assumes that this is the case, saying: 'God said to me …' 'God answered me …,' whereas it is not so at all, but, as we have said, it is for the most part they who are saying it to themselves."[55]

[55] *Ascent of Mount Carmel*, bk. 2, ch. 24.

True or False Possession?

The superego, which is made out to be some kind of entity, really corresponds only to a function, which cannot be materialized in such an oversimplified form. To say with Rosette Dubal that we project the superego externally under the form of the double, and that this doubling is what we find in all cases of possession and hallucination, is a picturesque metaphor, but no more. If the psychological mechanism invoked by the psychoanalytic school were the real source of pseudo-diabolical possession, one would wonder why this deviation of the mind is not more common and why this singular disturbance affects only a certain category of individuals.

In short, psychoanalysis dresses up what we already knew with picturesque and easily grasped images, but we shall be deceived if we look for the secret of demonopathy in the concepts of psychoanalysis.

Psychological Possession

We cannot be surprised to learn or confirm that many minds that have received an advanced scientific education refuse to believe in the possibility of demoniacal possession, such as was observed in the Middle Ages. I would go further: many believers seem very annoyed when they are questioned on the validity of the medieval conception of diabolical possession.

It is, no doubt, some such reason that has led a man like Marcel de la Bigne de Villeneuve to imagine a dialogue like those of the Encyclopedists, in which two speakers take part, apparently but not really opposed, and both evidently believers. Somewhat disappointed by the incompleteness of the *Satan* published by the *Études Carmélitaines,* and desiring to clarify his faith in the reality of the devil by a thorough knowledge of genuine demoniacal possession, this author imagines himself consulting an expert theologian, Abbé Multi. Does not our conception of the evil one, he asks, give a handle to many critics? Can they not reproach us with giving life to pure abstractions, with actualizing hypostases in order to make our discourses comprehensible? Is it not the plain truth that Lucifer and all the millions of devils over which he reigns are quite simply the personification of our evil tendencies and our vices?

"Your critics," declares Abbé Multi, "are either ignorant or imbecile." Now we know what our theologian would have us think of the psychoanalysis of the devil! Continuing his demonstration, the abbé professes that the state of true possession "testifies to an intense psychomotor disturbance and reveals the complete dissociation of the personality, in which a hostile external control is substituted for the normal individual control of ideas and actions."[56]

The devil can, no doubt, take the human form, but it is by no means impossible for him to clothe himself in material or immaterial objects. Thus the Prince of Darkness disguises himself willingly, or even preferably, under the appearance *of corporate personalities or institutions.*

The idea of a general obsession, occult and invisible, or of a collective, political and social possession, does in fact help us to explain more easily the rarity of individual diabolical possessions in contemporary society. "The violent, physical inhabitation [of the demon] is less and less useful to the enemy of the human race." "In place of a spectacular occupation, always liable to provoke vehement reactions, he can advantageously substitute the simple occupation of minds and souls, calmer and

[56]Marcel de la Bigne de Villeneuve, *Satan dans la Cité* (Paris: Ed. du Cedré, 1951), p. 43.

more insinuating but no less sure, fitted for a more rapid contagion and the widest possible diffusion."[57]

While rejecting the opinion of Simone Weil, that "the social is irreducibly the domain of the devil," and also that the
devil is "the father of all kinds of prestige, and prestige is social,"
the learned theologian avows himself convinced that "the social milieu is eminently fitted for demoniacal infestation." It is
evident that our doctor has been trained in the modern psychological discipline, according to which (and nothing seems
better verified) there are no strictly individual facts. Whether
one accepts it willingly or unwillingly, the doctrines, theories,
actions, and tendencies of an epoch are constituted and modeled under the forces of social pressure.

In the world of life, as well as in the physical field, there is
no completely isolated event. Satan no longer appears as a personage, an isolated figure, but rather as an essence insinuating
itself craftily into the hearts of certain states, in order to corrupt
them by the sin of pride, "for pride is always seen to be the essential base of the diabolic."

It follows, therefore, that we may hold that Hitlerite Ger-
many, which "contained good, useful, and even excellent elements," found itself terribly dominated by the influence of the
devil.

We may remark that this interpretation is only, in brief, the
development of the theory expounded by Dom Aloïs Mager in
some brilliant pages in the *Satan* of the *Études Carmélitaines*. If
the Christian is convinced that evil consists essentially in the
lust of the flesh, that is, of the senses, in the lust of knowledge,
and the lust of domination, the pride of life—*libido sentiendi,*

[57]La Bigne de Villeneuve, *Satan dans la Cité*, 69-70.

libido cognoscendi, libido dominandi—he must agree that the Nazi society was specially fitted for the growth and hypertrophy of these three modes of concupiscence.

Dom Aloïs Mager, who lived in this vitiated atmosphere, therefore considered Hitler to be the medium of Satan. "No one who is not deluded could see in Hitler a great personality either from the point of view of character or of morality." General Jodl said of him at the Nuremberg trial: "He was a great man, but an infernal great man." Given over to lying, he pretends to develop and cultivate relations with the Holy See, but to his intimates he speaks thus about the Christians: "I know how to treat these people in order to reduce them. They will either bend or be broken, and since they are not animals, they will bend." To fight the Church one must beware of making martyrs; it must be withered up.[58]

With Hitler we may compare Alastair Crowley, "the most unclean and perverted man in Britain," in Mr. Justice's words. When questioned on his identity, Crowley replied: "Before Hitler was, I am." The ritual of black magic was practiced at his grave; his followers chanted diabolical incantations: the "Hymn to Pan," by Crowley; the "Hymn to Satan," by Giosuè Carducci.

Finally I recall that the British press referred in 1948 to a report, produced by Harry Price, a celebrated demonologist, under the aegis of London University, which reveals that in all districts of London there are hundreds of men and women, of excellent education and intellect and high social position, who worship the devil and offer him a regular cultus. "Black magic, witchcraft, invocation of the devil, these three forms of

[58]See *Satan*, 639. English trans., 501.

medieval superstition, are practised today in London on a scale and with a freedom unknown in the Middle Ages."

The scale of this work does not permit of further investigation: the literature of the nineteenth and twentieth centuries affords us numerous examples testifying to the importance ascribed to the devil's influence on the body social, by novelists, poets, and writers in general. And it is worth noting that on this subject the preeminence belongs without question to French authors and to the Russian novelists, the greatest of whom is Dostoyevsky.

But if we grant that the universal influence and penetration of the devil among the collective bodies is probable and predominant, must we therefore deny that the devil can disguise himself very cleverly, in the most cunning manner, in some "master of thought"? This is the problem that M. Pierre Bontang sets himself to solve.[59]

"There are people who believe that Jean-Paul Sartre is the devil in person," writes this author in the first lines of his book. "No, he is not, and to put a stop to any wrong interpretation, I shall say that Jean-Paul Sartre is not the final form of the devil (a reputation which might displease both); I shall try to prove that he is nothing of the sort, but that there is still a relationship between the two: that of possession." Briefly, it is not Sartre who possesses the devil, but the demon which is in him.

What reasons move Bontang to accept the idea, too obvious to simple minds, that Jean-Paul Sartre is a genuine case of demoniacal possession? First, that while Sartre well describes the abandonment, the dereliction of man on the earth, and the

---

[59]P. Bontang, *Sartre est il un possédé?* (Paris: La Table Ronde, 1950)

anguish that grips him, his thought has no surrounding fringe of effectivity. In contrast with Jaspers, Kierkegaard, and Heidegger, the author or *Being and Non-being* seems to have no conception that things can be comprehended, not only with one's reason but with one's heart. "The heart has its reasons," too, which Sartre knows not. Atheist existentialism, by repudiating all lyricism, reduces the human condition to nothing but "a little true fact." Man, dispossessed of God, now knows that he can count only on himself. In the vacuum left by the divine dispossession, may there not be established a real possession, which gives the explanation of his whole work?

To the problem of the existence of God Sartre replies: "No question exists, it is just so, it is quite simple." Even if God existed, it would make no difference: the dereliction would still be there, and as full of anguish.

In Bontang's view, what separates the sinner from the possessed lies chiefly in this proposition: the sinner finds himself confronted with the fact of his sin; he glides along with it, being connected with it. In the possessed man, on the contrary, evil is substituted for his personality, and "all transcendence establishing the relation of a real subject to the fact of the sin, keeping them face-to-face, is abolished. The subject has disappeared. There is nothing left but the evil which is its guest."

I have mentioned this theory of Pierre Bontang's, about a writer whose intelligence and critical spirit, no less than the depth and extent of his knowledge, are beyond question, only in order to show how far astray a man can be led, lacking a "clear and distinct" notion of possession. The possessed person, whether genuine or not, can retain a perfectly clear notion of his guilt, his sins. He is not in the least a mere envelope of evil; his conduct is far from automatic, although he cannot always master it. Finally, he who believes in the devil believes in God, but here we are very far from Jean-Paul Sartre, and from all the atheist philosophers to whom destiny has refused that indefinable gift, that perfume of the spirit which is Charity.

Conclusion

As I have tried to show, from the events of history or from my own observation, there can be no doubt that, even in the present age, when science has shown that so many facts which seemed to our fathers incomprehensible and beyond nature were natural phenomena, many persons have all the appearance of being possessed by the evil spirit, the demon, or Satan.

What is the truth of the matter? Ought we to accept as real the diabolical possession of which the New Testament gives so many examples? And if there can be no doubt of the existence of non-genuine possessions, are we in a position to distinguish them from the genuine? Do we possess criteria that prevent us from going astray? To a great extent, an affirmative answer can be given.

When, in actual fact, a delirium of demonopathic possession develops, under our observation, according to the same laws that condition a delirium similar in all respects except color and content; when the same therapeutic treatment proves capable of reducing both kinds, then we must be convinced that the disorder is one whose cause is to be found, not in "supernature," but in nature itself, nature spoiled by a morbid process.

If, on the contrary, the phenomena of possession appear only in a parasitic capacity, or are accompanied by very high qualities of mind and heart, then the doctor must call in the qualified theologian, the exorcist. There should be no need to add that when the subject of the supposed possession belongs to a religious community or order, it is for the religious superiors to carry out the first examination and to decide on the case.

One last question for the theorist: When the devil enters into a man's soul and body, can he reveal his presence exclusively by the semblance of a mental or bodily illness? In other words, when the doctor recognizes in a patient all the elements of a definite disease, has he the right to see in it *only* the effects of a natural process, even when a scientific treatment is able to cure it?

It is not for me to resolve this problem and on this point the reader must form his own judgment according to his beliefs.

Select Bibliography

Alexander, W. M. *Demoniac Possession in the New Testament.* Edinburgh: Clark, 1902.

Biot, René. *The Riddle of the Stigmata.* London: Burns and Oates, 1962.

Bruno de Jesus-Marie, O.C.D., ed. *Satan.* London and New York: Sheed and Ward, 1951. (This collection of essays — a translation from the French of the *Études Carmélitaines* volume published in 1948 — by various authorities provides an exhaustive treatment of the subject with full references.)

Corte, Nicolas. *Who Is the Devil?* New York: Hawthorn Books, 1958; Manchester, New Hampshire: Sophia Institute Press, 2013.

Cristiani, L. *Satan in the Modern World.* Translated by C. Rowland. London: Barrie and Rockliff, 1961.

Huxley, Aldous. *The Devils of Loudun.* London: Chatto and Windus, and New York, Harper, 1952.

John of the Cross, St. *The Complete Works of St. John of the Cross*. Translated and edited by E. Allison Peers from the Critical Edition of P. Silverio de Santa Teresa, C.D. 3 Vols. London: Burns and Oates, and Westminster, Maryland: Newman Press, 1953.

Kelly, Bernard J. *God, Man and Satan*. Westminster, Maryland: Newman Press, 1951.

Knox, Ronald A. *Enthusiasm*. London and New York: Oxford University Press, 1950 (especially chapter 15).

Langton, Edward. *Essentials of Demonology*. London: Epworth Press and Naperville, Illinois: Allenson, 1949.

———. *Good and Evil Spirits*. London: Epworth Press, 1942.

———. *Satan, a Portrait*. London: Epworth Press, and New York: Macmillan, 1946.

Murray, M. A. *The Witch-Cult in Western Europe*. Oxford: Clarendon Press, and New York: Oxford University Press, 1921.

Oesterreich, T. *Possession, Demoniacal and Other*. London, Kegan Paul, 1950.

Reginald-Omez, Fr., O.P. *Psychical Phenomena*. London: Burns and Oates, 1959.

Schlier, H. *Principalities and Powers in the New Testament*. London and New York: Nelson, 1961.

Sheppard, Lancelot C. *Barbe Acarie, Wife and Mystic*. London: Burns and Oates, and New York: McKay, 1953.

Strauss, E. B. *Psychiatry in the Modern World*. London, Michael Joseph, 1958.

Teresa of Jesus, St. *The Complete Works of St. Teresa of Jesus*. Translated and edited by E. Allison Peers. London and New York: Sheed and Ward, 1946.

———. *The Letters of St. Teresa of Jesus*. Translated and edited by E. Allison Peers from the Critical Edition of P. Silverio de Santa Teresa, C.D., 3 Vols. London: Burns and Oates, 1951, and Westminster, Maryland: Newman Press, 1952.

Thurston, Herbert, S.J. *Ghosts and Poltergeists*. London: Burns and Oates, 1953.

———. *The Physical Phenomena of Mysticism*. London: Burns and Oates, and Chicago: Regnery, 1951.

———. *Surprising Mystics*. London: Burns and Oates, and Chicago: Regnery, 1955.

Wiesinger, Alois. *Occult Phenomena in the Light of Theology*. London, Burns and Oates, and Westminster, Maryland: Newman Press, 1957.

Williams, Charles. *Witchcraft*. London: Faber and Faber, 1941.

An Invitation

Reader, the book that you hold in your hands was published by Sophia Institute Press.

Sophia Institute seeks to restore man's knowledge of eternal truth, including man's knowledge of his own nature, his relation to other persons, and his relation to God.

Our press fulfills this mission by offering translations, reprints, and new publications. We offer scholarly as well as popular publications; there are works of fiction along with books that draw from all the arts and sciences of our civilization. These books afford readers a rich source of the enduring wisdom of mankind.

Sophia Institute Press also serves as the publisher for the Thomas More College of Liberal Arts and Holy Spirit College. Both colleges are dedicated to providing university-level education in the Western tradition under the guiding light of Catholic teaching.

If you know a young person who might be interested in the ideas found in this book, share it. If you know a young person seeking a college that takes seriously the adventure of learning and the quest for truth, bring our institutions to his attention.

www.SophiaInstitute.com
www.ThomasMoreCollege.edu
www.HolySpiritCollege.org

SOPHIA INSTITUTE PRESS

THE PUBLISHING DIVISION OF

THOMAS MORE COLLEGE
of LIBERAL ARTS   HOLY SPIRIT COLLEGE